think Believe Receive

think Believe Receive

TM

Think, Believe, Receive

—Three steps to An Amazing Life—

BRIAN K. GRAHAM

BALBOA.
PRESS

A DIVISION OF HAY HOUSE

Balboa Press books may be ordered through booksellers or by contacting:

Balboa Press
A Division of Hay House
1663 Liberty Drive
Bloomington, IN 47403
www.balboapress.com
1-(877) 407-4847

ISBN: 978-1-4525-3362-9 (sc)
ISBN: 978-1-4525-3364-3 (hc)
ISBN: 978-1-4525-3363-6 (e)

Library of Congress Control Number: 2011904619

Printed in the United States of America

Balboa Press rev. date: 4/08/2011

Contents

Dedication

This book is dedicated to my entire family beginning with my wonderful wife Cheryl, without whom my life is incomplete. Also Mindy, Becky M, Sara, Adam, Billy, Becky G, and especially my grandchildren who opened my heart to finding a deeper understanding of life.

I also want to thank all my editors and readers who have given their time and offered invaluable suggestions to make TBR clearer to future readers.

And of course, thanks to the developer of the idea behind Think, Believe, Receive: Gayle Rock whose vision inspired this book.

Introduction

I want to challenge you right now. The challenge is to create the life you really want to experience. Not the life your parents wanted for you, not the life you think your significant other wants you to experience, society, or anyone or anything else wants you to experience. The life YOU want to experience.

I am going to go out on a limb here and suggest the life you want to experience does not include physical discomfort, mental anguish, financial hardships or feeling alone. I am further more going to suggest that no matter what you have, think or do, regardless of how this appears to yourself or others, you have an even greater dream for your life which you may be reluctant to express to others, or even to yourself.

The good news which is this creative process of Think, Believe, Receive, is that you can have everything you want. I mean that literately, you can have everything you want simply through the proper use of three simple steps: Think, Believe, Receive.

This is not a new idea. This isn't some New Age airy-fairy concept. This is the truth and it is active in your being right now. What you are experiencing right now is a result of how you process your thoughts. What you are experiencing right now is a direct reflection of your thoughts. It's that simple. The key to having the life you envision for yourself, the things you want in your life is how you think, what you believe and how willing you are to receive the good that is yours right now.

You are a creative being. From the very first moment you processed your first thought you have been creating your experience. The thing is; you may not have been aware of what you were creating or aware of how those thoughts have manifested in your life.

Think of it: when you were a baby, if you were hungry or wanted your diaper changed all you had to do was cry and someone arrived with food or a fresh diaper. This was a wonderful system with two steps: step one: need and demand, step two: fulfillment.

As a toddler you carried this understanding forward. Cry then get. But soon your range of desires expanded beyond food or diaper changes and no longer did crying necessarily result in receiving what you wanted, so a new communication method was required; talking. Baby talk worked for awhile, your parents even thought it was cute and you got your needs fulfilled. But sooner or later "they" insisted you learn to communicate "their" way. No longer was it sufficient to say "I Want" and you got it. Gradually you came to understand this life was not all about YOU. Someone might even have taught you that you were not the center of the Universe. Is it any wonder that as we reach adolescence we rebel and act out? All we are doing is trying to reclaim that wonderful time when life was Ask, and it is Given; the freedom and immediate response we experienced in our infancy. Before we knew it we were socialized to question our very worthiness to even have!

All this, of course, was done with the best of intentions by "them" so we could 'fit into society'. In time this socialization resulted in anger, frustration, fear and doubt, but again, most of us learned to repress these feelings as well, because expressing them was not 'fitting into society.'

To conform, and 'fit-in' some of us slipped into nine to five jobs we hated, really only living from Friday night until Monday morning and simply existing the other five days. Some of us drifted from job to job looking for fulfillment from things and experiences outside ourselves because the Ask and it is Given option had been closed with the phrase "grow-up". Some of us took refuge in drugs, alcohol or other behaviors which, no matter how diligently we tried, still left us feeling empty.

We have all heard the stories about the guy who worked at the same job for thirty years, never missed a day, retired, got a gold watch, went home and six months later was dead because along with loosing his defined position in a company, also lost his personal identity. In truth, he had given-over his true nature in favor of 'fitting-in.'

These examples of life, from earliest experience to final experience demonstrate the action of choice we all have and use all the time. Unfortunately we use this choice without being aware we are doing so.

As we have said: we are creative beings. Creating all the time, receiving what we have created, yet unaware we have used our native power to choose, and blind to the realization that we have gotten what we requested. That is a tremendously powerless place to be.

But, what if, what if we became fully conscious of ourselves making those choices? What if we recognized our choices were always answered by a power unlimited in nature, and what if we were awakened to those choices those demands, as they arrived in our experience? And, what if when we realized that if those choices and their arrival did not fill us with the joy which is our natural state of being- we could choose again and have a different experience without guilt, anxiety or fear? Wouldn't that feel better?

The good news is that is just how our universe works, always has, always will. The key to successfully working this system is being conscious of our own part in the creative process. We are not pawns in the scheme of things; we are masters of our own reality- if we choose to step up to the plate.

This is exactly what Think, Believe, Receive is all about. It is about YOU taking charge of YOUR life, YOU taking responsibility for YOUR experience, YOU coming from a place of happiness and joy because YOU realize your own part in your experience. Think, Believe, Receive is about YOU becoming conscious, fully conscious.

Regardless of your religious training or indoctrination, your place in society, or economic standing YOU and only YOU are in charge of what you experience in this life. What we are going to do here is go back to infancy and get back to the simple way of life; Ask and it is Given, Need/fulfillment. We will explore how to reconnect our physical experience with Creative Force which is the Source of our power. Creative Force is the name we have chosen to use in this book: you may call It God, All There Is, First Cause, The Universe, even Chuck if you wish. It does not care about names and words, It only loves.

First, however you must accept yourself as a creative powerhouse, then Think, Believe, Receive.

I open myself to possibility, knowing I do so of my own free
will and with the power of the Universe to support me.

THINK

Watch your thoughts for they become words, watch your
words for they become actions. Watch your actions for they
become habits. Watch your habits for they become character.
Watch your character for it becomes your destiny.
(anon)

A man's private thought can never be a lie.
What he thinks is, to him, the truth, always.
(Mark Twain)

From thought all things are begun.
(Brian Graham)

Act or Re-Act

The socialization process each of us has undergone serves many wonderful purposes; it allows us to move about society behaving in a manner which permits us to earn a living, be part of a social group, and be with others in a more or less peaceful manner. Each social group has its own codes and mores; rules if you will, which define how we must behave, dress, eat and so much more.

If, for instance you happen to be an outlaw biker, chances are your clothing runs toward denim pants, vest, unruly hair, larger physique, tattoos and perhaps a tendency toward a slightly aggressive behavior toward others. Your dining choices probably run toward hand-held foods, free of the encumbrances of plates, silverware and napkins, and your speech most likely contains a salty array of language. Now could you envision an outlaw biker in a three piece suit, matching tie and a two hundred dollar hair cut, manicured and wafting the scent of fine cologne? No, that probably wouldn't fit the image and mores of the group.

This of course is a broad characterization of a specific group of people which may or may not fit everyone in that group, but this is what we have come to accept and expect of outlaw bikers.

Would you be surprised to learn that many of the motorcycles outlaw bikers ride cost in the tens of thousands of dollars each? That the biker next to you in traffic with denims, vest and unruly hair is actually an attorney or doctor or business man or woman who earns more than the gross national product of many smaller nations?

You see, our socialization process has set up in us a whole set of expectations based on clothing, houses, possessions and the activities in which we engage. When we see someone dressed in jeans with a big chopper we act a certain way. Perhaps we move away from them, roll up our windows, lock the doors, or, maybe we flash them a thumbs up. We take action based upon our training, but what we are doing is not acting at all, what we are doing is RE-ACTING; behaving in a manner consistent with what we have been taught, or experienced at *another time and place.*

If my son comes to me and says "Dad, can I have $200.00?" I have two choices. I can Act or Re-Act. If I choose to Re-Act my response might be "I gave you $200.00 last month, do you think money grows on trees?" This is Re-Acting based upon what happened before, not action based on what is happening now. If I choose to Act, I might ask why he needs the money and evaluate the request on its merits today, now, the situation at hand.

So let's say I Re-Acted, blew him off then I come to learn he needs the money because he spent all he has for text books and needs a loan for a week to cover his rent, now wouldn't I feel foolish? I want him to get an education and I want him to have a safe place to live. The best place for both of us is for me to come from the place of *Action*, rather than *Re-Action.*

Re-Action shuts the door to our greater good. When we live our lives from the Re-Act place we have limited what good can come to us because we are saying to ourselves "I know everything, I have experienced everything, and nothing good can come from change." To Re-Act is to come from fear; fear of change, fear of losing something, fear of revealing some short-coming we feel about ourselves. Being in Re-Action is not coming from our place of power; it is not coming from the place of possible.

Through the use of Think, Believe, Receive, we are now in the business of making *conscious* choices about our lives. It is possible that closing the windows and locking the doors when a threatening visage appears in your vicinity is the right and proper choice. It is possible that denying a loan is the right choice at the moment. What is most important here is to make our choices based upon NOW, the situation as it is right here, rather than automatically going to the default setting of Re-Action and relying on what someone else told us is right or what we perceived from another experience.

As creative beings it is essential we become aware that we are making choices. This is the first step to our empowerment. If we are not at choice, if we must live our lives as we have always lived our lives, never expanding, never growing, never being in a position to experience the Unlimited in our lives, we are not living at all, we are just taking up space.

ACT according to the possibility which is today. Be aware YOU are at choice. If the choice you make results in something you don't like, , next time you are free to choose a different path.

Today I am aware of my choices. I choose to act
from the highest and best in all I do.

The "R" Word

One of my wonderful teachers, Reverend Marylou Sergeant, used to tell me that people are really afraid of the "R" word. The "R" word to which she referred is Responsibility.

What's the big deal? Why do we shy away from responsibility? We think it is because we confuse the idea of responsibility with the concept of blame. No one wants to take the blame because blame implies wrong-doing, malfeasance, perhaps even criminal intent! Taking the blame means we did something wrong; we are lacking, less than worthy. Blame is a word filled with unpleasant connotations. It is no surprise, therefore, that there is such resistance to taking the blame, but blame and responsibility are not the same thing at all.

Sometimes things happen we do not anticipate, things don't turn out the way we think they should have, but rather than place BLAME we might want to identify responsibility. When the local professional basketball team doesn't perform well are the fans to blame? Is the cause of their poor performance someone's responsibility? Yes, but not the fans.   In identifying who or what is responsible for a less than stellar season for the team we open the door to better results in the future. Blame makes us (or someone else) wrong, and when we feel someone wants to make us wrong we naturally go into a defensive posture to protect ourselves. This is a simple example of what we have already identified as Re-Action. From this Re-Action place the next step is to find someone else to lay the blame upon. This becomes a vicious cycle which is the exact opposite of what we want to build here: a better result next time through conscious choices.

Picture yourself driving home, minding your own business, perhaps planning dinner or some work around the house. Suddenly you realize you have run a stop sign. You realize this because in your rear-view mirror is a motorcycle cop with his lights flashing. Fifteen minutes later you are driving away with a ticket, a substantial fine, a point on your driving record, and a bad attitude. "If that cop hadn't been there everything would have been fine", you say to yourself. You are blaming the cop for your actions, casting yourself in the role of victim. Blaming the cop seems to ease the sting of the ticket, but very soon the salve of blame morphs into the irritant of victim hood. In victim hood we are powerless: we have no power to change our future actions, no power to do things differently. We become subject to "them", subject to their whims. It is only by accepting Personal Responsibility that we reclaim our power to shape our behavior, and in doing so, shape our future. In changing our thinking from victim hood to personal responsibility we adopt the power to change our lives.

Perhaps this equation will make this concept even clearer:

Blame=fault=bad=powerlessness.
Personal Responsibility= Personal Power= Possibility

As we live our lives from the perspective of possibility we free ourselves to experience all the good we want to have in our lives.

This book is called Think, Believe, Receive and the first step to receiving is always THINK. THINK your life can be better, THINK you are a worthy part of a Universe which wants you to be happy,

THINK that happiness is possible and not only possible, but yours for the creating.

What you THINK produces tangible results in every aspect of our lives which is why we want to move away from blame and take personal responsibility for all our actions, thoughts and words.

The "R" word. Accept it, use it, and free yourself!

I accept responsibility for my words and actions in every situation. I am responsible for my life.

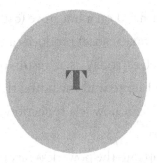

Cause and Effect

How many times have you looked at your life situation and asked yourself, "How did I get here?" Almost certainly this question does not arise because something life-affirming has occurred. Most often that question arises because we have found ourselves in a hole of some kind. As a wise person once said: "when you find yourself in a hole, STOP DIGGING!"

Perhaps our relationship is on the rocks, or our financial situation is precarious, maybe our health is not what we want it to be. As we have already discussed, blaming ourselves or others for our experience will not be helpful here at all. We will not be in a position to change what is happening to us if we blame others because where we are now, what we are experiencing, has nothing to do with our idiot husband or the employer who refuses to give us a pay raise. Everything we experience is the result of our way of thinking, so change your thinking, and stop digging the hole deeper! Now, this is a challenging idea at first, still it remains the one and only way to get out of that hole.

Every one of us is operating in a universe which is governed by a Law of Cause and Effect. If we do this, that will happen. If we think this, we will feel that. There is no escaping this Law. Physics teaches us a body in motion (cause) tends to stay in motion (effect). Experience teaches us if we put our hand on a hot stove (cause) we will get burned (effect). Each action we take (cause) produces a reaction (effect).

How we see ourselves today is a result of every thought and experience we have had up to and including this very moment. Even our physical condition right now is a reflection of what we have done and thought in our past.

Now, before we jump into the powerless pity pool of blame and guilt let's quickly move to the position of power: If what I am experiencing right now is a result of my thinking, then I can change this experience by changing my thinking. Furthermore: I could have not gotten to this place of understanding, this place of power without having had these experiences, so I do not have to carry guilt forward with me! Suddenly we are out of victim-hood and into power and possible. This is a subtle but very important shift in our thinking which will immediately alter our experience. This too is Cause and Effect.

One of the clearest first steps we can take to bring more joy, more love, more prosperity and more peace into our lives, and at the same time eliminate the power from the question "How did I get here?" is to accept we have absolutely no power over what others think.

So often we find ourselves dissatisfied with our lives because we believe we have done nothing but serve others- do what others want. "I have given everything to (fill in the name), dedicated myself to this job, and gotten nothing back." If we live our lives trying to be what we think others want us to be or do, we inevitably create resentment within our own lives. In addition to harboring this resentment, we are living our lives out of personal integrity. Seeking affirmation of our worthiness from others can only lead to our own dissatisfaction because there is never, never, never enough outside affirmation to fill our inner being, and we cannot control what others think, no matter how many hours we put in at the job. Once again the question: "How did I get here?" Answer: I created this place for myself.

Well documented medical studies suggest up to 75% of all medical conditions are the result of our thinking. Those who harbor resentment and unforgiveness have a far higher experience of stress related physical symptoms such as ulcers, insomnia and even cancers. The Law of Cause and Effect is in play here, and manifests even through our bodies.

Those who live their lives in service to others because they find joy inside themselves for their work experience far fewer illnesses- illnesses from colds to cancer. There is a direct and clear relationship between how we think and what our life looks like.

Our words have power, and so do our thoughts. Our words and thoughts set the Universe in motion to produce specific results. Our thoughts set an emotional stage upon which our world performs.

Let's use some examples to illustrate this idea: If my thought is "all the waitresses in this place are incompetent fools." The result is no matter how flawlessly my waitress does her job, no matter how impeccable the service is, I will find some way to justify my thought; I will find something I can call incompetence. I set my stage and the world performs upon it while I do the critique.

"My wife never listens to what I say" shows up in my life with continual proof of my thought, regardless of ample evidence to the contrary.

"No one appreciates what I do" sets the stage for me to ignore any and all evidence to the contrary.

We set the stage in our minds, we are the directors of the play, we are the critics of our own experience and we are the readers of our own reviews. It is a closed circle we can alter at any of these junctures simply by changing how we think about things.

Now, what if we change the question from "why does my life stink?" to what is good in my life?

From this place of power the world begins to shift and it will shift quickly. Here are some suggestions for steps you might try:

1) Accept you have no control over anybody else's thoughts, feelings or actions. You only have control over your own thoughts, feelings and actions.

2) Accept that no one goes around saying "how can I annoy (your name here) today. The truth is everyone is concerned primarily with their own personal experience. Don't take it personally, but you don't even come into the equation..

3) Allow yourself to remember at any given moment you and everyone else is doing the best they can at that moment. Ten minutes later they may do the same thing differently, but this moment, this choice; it's the best you or they can do now.

4) Allow yourself to forgive. Forgiveness is the most important step to self-empowerment, and joy. If at any given moment you are doing the best you can do, and at any given moment everyone else is doing the best they can do; right and wrong, good and bad are simply perceptions. All we can do is the best we can do. Forgive yourself and forgive others.

5) Remember, your perceptions are your creation. You are totally in control of your own responses. Allow that power to be your guiding force in every interaction.

6) Release yourself from the judgment of others and of yourself. (We will explore judgment in a later chapter).

Our life today is indeed the result of how we have been thinking, therefore if there is something in our lives we would like to experience differently; all we have to do is change our thinking.

My thinking is the cause, my experience is the effect. I am at power to change both through my thinking, and I do so beginning right now.

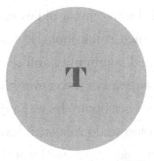

Now, Now, Now

As we embark upon this journey to a more powerful experience, it is essential to embrace the truth that any meaningful change can only take place right now. Yesterday is in the books, even what happened a second ago is done- stick a fork in it. Tomorrow, including a nano-second from now is yet to be written. That means the only place for change is NOW. Someday never comes. It is always now.

"Someday I will learn to play tennis."

"Someday I will make peace with my sister."

"Someday I will (insert action here)."

When we say someday we set up a situation we never have to face because when is someday? It is no-day.

"I wish I had never met you."

"I wish I had done things differently"

"I wish I had never said that."

The truth remains the truth and the past remains the past. You did that thing, you met that person, you said those words, and so what are you going to do NOW? What you are going to do is to begin right NOW to move on. It is the only thing you can do and the only time you can do it is NOW.

NOW is our power, NOW is the beginning, NOW is the possible.

I was called recently by an 84 year old woman (let's call her Joyce) whose husband had turned to alcohol. He had moved out of their beautiful home in a gated community and she was afraid he would return to harm her (or worse). For Joyce, everything in her life seemed trashed. As I walked into her home she was a quivering mass of fear, shaking like a leaf; sleepless and exhausted. Joyce's entire life seemed to be weighing on her shoulders, and with good reason. Joyce was out of her NOW. She was devastated at her husbands choices, crushed he had left her, afraid of what might happen in the future, terrified as to her own prospects for the remainder of her days. She had not slept or eaten in days. Joyce had clearly given away her only place of power, her NOW.

Putting new locks on the doors was not my first priority. Securing the windows from forced entry was secondary. My first priority was to help her find her own way back to her place of power, a place where things could change. These changes could not take place in the past, these changes could not wait until the future, they could only happen in the NOW.

After listening to her story (and only once through because her story is about the past) we began breaking the whole ugly situation into what could be done NOW to help ease her fear. It's true our goal was a future sense of security, but that security tomorrow had to begin this moment because, again, tomorrow never comes. We only have the NOW.

Acting in the NOW, we contacted the community security force and asked for regular welfare checks which immediately reduced her level of fear. Next we contacted her accountant to see what could be done to insure the security of her financial assets, and took action on what we could at that moment. Then we took a walk through her home to identify what measures could eliminate her concern about a potential forced entry. Within half an hour Joyce was a different person because she had taken all the NOW steps she could take. Rather than living and breathing her life from what had happened, or what might happen, our discussions and action steps brought us to the NOW, the only place of power Joyce, you or I have. As I left her home less than an hour later Joyce was ready sleep for the first time in several days.

I tell this story not to demonstrate my own brilliance, this story is about Joyce being willing to accept her own power and take back control of her life at the only point she could, in the NOW. She could just as easily have chosen to remain remorseful and powerless about what had happened yesterday, or last week or last year, but she was willing to return to where she could really do something, in the NOW. Joyce could also have chosen to dwell on what *might* occur, and this is an even richer field of dreams because the future, what might happen, is unfettered by fact, it is bounded only by imagination. You have probably been told "it's never as bad as it could be" which is true because we can construct every manner of ill unhampered by time, space or physical possibility! The future possibilities are unlimited, both for our good and our detriment.

In any stress filled experience our first step in returning to the wonderful, powerful creations we are, is to dissect the whole situation and break it down into smaller pieces with which we can work. Once we have manageable pieces we can then deal with them one at a time asking ourselves "what can I do NOW to resolve this issue?" Piece by piece, step by step, that is how the pyramids were built. Piece by piece, step by step, that is how an antiquated building is demolished, and fear lives in us as an antiquated building.

Within you is a magnificent being which far surpasses the majesty of the pyramids, and you can experience that magnificent being, but only if you change your thinking from living in the past or fearing the future, to being in the NOW.

Within you are experiences, memories, old conditioning, all manner of thoughts which no longer serve you, yet they still impact how you see yourself. These too can be released as you change your thinking to the power of the NOW.

The health you seek, the money you want in your life, the relationships you dream about, the peace of mind which is your natural way of being is yours if, and only if you change your thinking about your self, and the time to do that is NOW, NOW, NOW.

My power is in the now. I accept that every change I wish to see in my life can only begin right NOW.

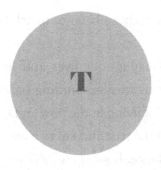

Balance

"All things in moderation." How many times have we heard that phrase?

When we are told to "Eat a balanced diet", or the story of Goldilocks and the Three Bears, these are both all about balance too! Chair not too big or too small, porridge not too hot or too cold, bed not too hard or too soft, just right! Balance!

The commandment to seek and live in balance has been part of our lives since childhood; still we often forget to make the connection of the importance of balance to our everyday lives. Balance is what nature is all about. Too much iron in the lawn turns it yellow, too little, it dies, the right amount results in a magnificent, lush green oasis in our yards.

If I spend too much time studying for my degree, my wife will feel excluded from my life. But wait a moment, if I get more education won't I be able to earn more money for both of us, provide a better lifestyle? Yes and no. If my wife's feelings of exclusion grows too great there will be no 'us' to enjoy that lifestyle, just two 'me's' and two lawyers. If fruit is good for me, but I eat too much I will grow just as plump as I would overindulging on chocolate cake. Exercise is good, but let it get out of balance and results in orthopedic surgery.

All of life is about striking a balance to achieve the most fulfilling experience.

The process of re-shaping our lives and letting Think, Believe, Receive truly work for us involves finding balance in ourselves. We have discussed the idea of living in the now and how that empowers us, yet if we forget to honor the past and fail to have dreams for our future, we are living out of balance. If we spend all our time trying to predict what the cause and effect of this action or that action, we will be like deer in the headlights, unable to do anything. It is the same thing if we insist on accepting responsibility for everyone else's actions, we are out of balance. Regardless of the purity of intentions or worthiness of their concepts, anyone who allows any one part of their lives to overwhelm the others will certainly find themselves out of balance, accomplishing nothing at all.

Why then is balance so important to the creative process of Think, Believe, Receive? Because at this stage of our eternal lives we have both a physical and a spiritual component, and both aspects are designed to worth together to produce the maximum results. The person who views their body as the source of their power and possibility, tends to approach every challenge from the physical viewpoint. They will exclusively use their physical body in attempting to resolve life's experiences. This person may attempt to find joy in generating money through extended periods of work, or attempt to find joy exclusively in how their body appears. This is where we get the idea that "might makes right." Warfare is an example of this unbalanced thinking. If we can overwhelm our "enemy" we will win the conflict. This is simply not so. The United States threw overwhelming numbers of troops against the Viet Cong, yet lost the war because the powers that were did not factor in the will of our opponents. Through sheer determination, incredible feats of physical effort and spiritual dedication, the Viet Cong withstood the most powerful occupying force ever assembled.

Physical might does not make right, and it most often doesn't even win in the long run.

On the other end of the spectrum are those who wrap themselves in spirituality, secede from everyday life to live alone in contemplation and meditation. No doubt some of these folks do indeed re-discover the truth about their beings, that they are spiritual beings having a physical experience. No doubt some of these people even come to profound understandings about how physical humankind can come to terms with the deep mysteries of life, yet we are reminded, 'faith without works is dead'. Withdrawing from life in favor of spiritual experience exclusively is out of balance.

Mother Theresa is a prime example of balance in every day life. Surrounded by more need than she could physically fulfill she kept going because her power came from more than her physical being. Father Damien of the Hawaiian leper colony is another example of someone who gave his all in physical terms yet drew upon his spiritual self to help him do even more. The list is long, but what these notables displayed is the awareness of balance as their guiding principle. Physical works powered not by muscle or body alone, but powered and tempered by their spiritual aspect as well.

One may take any concept we set forth here and attempt to produce results by mind alone. They may attempt to think all these principles into being and demonstration only to become frustrated because the demonstrations are shallow or require massive amounts of effort. This is no fun and will only result in ultimate failure. We cannot stress enough, this process of Think, Believe, Receive, or any worthwhile endeavor for that matter, can only be successful when both the physical and spiritual aspects of our beings are in balance, working together. Without recognizing the underlying truth that we are extensions of a limitless source of power, and guidance, this whole process becomes simply a mental exercise, therefore, almost worthless.

You have a body, that is clear. What might not be as clear is that you also have a spiritual component as well. From this moment forward, let's consciously bring these two components together to create more than two halves, let us create something which is more than the sum of its parts. It matters not if you choose to call your spiritual component God, Jesus, All That Is, The Universe, The Cosmos, Love or even Chuck, the Creative Force which takes the power of our thought and words and converts them into physical stuff or experiences does not care either. Why should It? It is that It is.

Physical action or mental action alone cannot produce lasting, fulfilling results. It is only through the balanced merging of the physical and spiritual will what we seek become a reality. Regardless of the project at hand, don't begin the job with half your tools. Bring all your tools to the job and the results will be faster, more satisfying and longer lasting. Balance, it's what's for success!

Each moment, each action, each thought I have is
more powerful as I embrace balance in my life.

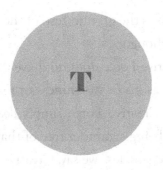

Picture It

With this book we are putting forth what might be a rather startling concept: to have what you want takes only three steps; Think, Believe, Receive. But how do we actually go about placing a demand on the Universe? First, speak your word for the good you desire (Think). Next we envision that good as being done and in your life now (Believe), then we allow the results into our lives (*Receive*). Exactly why does this think part work?

The truth is each and every moment of our lives we are thinking. That part is easy; the fact is we cannot refrain from putting out thoughts about things we want. If we have a cold, stuffy head, runny nose, cough, we are constantly putting out thoughts of freedom from these symptoms. If we go to pay the bills only to see fewer dollars in the checking account than the totals on the bills due, we are thinking we want more money. If we are assigned a project at work we would rather not undertake we may be thinking about how to get out of that project. We are always thinking, always placing demands on Creative Force.

Creative Force, for its part, always takes in our thoughts and words. It is powerless to do anything else, just as we are powerless to stop thinking. It is our nature to think, Its nature is to hear and respond in the affirmative. This is the ground zero of the creative process, and it all begins with our thoughts.

The thing is: Creative Force does not have a filter; Creative Force does not review our reasons or worthiness or make judgments about what we really want. Creative Force simply *does*. This is so simple when we think about being symptom free of that cold; "I want to get rid of these sneezes and sniffles" we say, Creative Force recognizes our demands and delivers. Depending upon our receptiveness to the relief, the manifestation can happen right now, or much later. "Ah" you say, "but statistics show that colds last for 7-10 days". That dear friend is 'medicine' speaking, not Creative Force. We will explore expectations in the following chapters, but whatever the reason, with clear intention and Creative Force working with you, you find yourself free from the symptoms in as little as an instant!

Now, about those bills which come in, sometimes it seems they come in faster than our apparent supply to pay them, now we get into some interesting stuff. "This is tangible," you say. "I have $2,000 dollars in bills and only $1,000 in my checkbook. This is real time, black and white, you can't deny that!" And, we won't deny that. What we will do is make a suggestion. Just as Joyce (in a previous chapter) was looking at her whole world in shambles because she was trying to deal with the entire experience at one time, and was unable to see the possibility around her, so too are you looking at the problem of $2,000 in bills versus $1,000 on hand: you are looking at the whole problem as a mountain rather than looking at it as a series of small bumps.

In this case, break the mountain down: change your thinking. If you don't think you can pay your bills, we promise you, you won't be able to pay them no matter how much cash you have on hand. You are broadcasting to Creative Force the idea you will not be able to pay your bills and Creative Force mirrors that belief right back to you, confirming there is no way to pay your bills. (This is another example of Cause and Effect). Break it down: the electric bill, that's due now, I can pay that. The gas bill, that's not due for two weeks, lets hold that one. Car payment, OK, I have enough for that one, and the grocery bill too. What we are now broadcasting to Creative Force is "I can find a way to do this", and what Creative Force is mirroring back to us and affirming is, we can find a way to do this. What this amounts to is simply changing the way we think about things, changing them into manageable bumps rather than a whole mountain. We are not denying at any point there is a financial aspect to this issue: with this change of thought we are simply opening ourselves to possible, to the unlimited.

Creative Force will always mirror our thoughts back to us, so if our thinking is of limitation, what we get back is limitation. Now, let's get back to those bills. We have opened ourselves to finding a way to pay them on time, so we offer that thought to Creative Force and what comes back? Perhaps an unanticipated bounty: an expense we expected turns out to not happen, we get a gift from someone which reduces another bill freeing up some money, the possibilities are endless because Creative Force is limitless in its ability to answer our demands. We are not depending upon luck or support from outside to meet our bills, we are relying on a limitless possibility ready to work with us as we alter our thought process to recognize It. This is Law in Action. Not Law in Action against you, Law in Action for you because you allowed it to work for you. Sometimes these happenstances like unplanned income or a lower bill than planned seem like miracles, but everything in the Cosmos is governed by the Law of Cause and Effect. If you expect limitation (cause) you experience limitation (effect). I don't even want to count the number of times I have looked at the expected bills for the month and then at the projected income for that month and wondered how it could work out, but by opening myself to possibility, by changing my thinking from limitation to possibility everything has gotten paid.

Anyone who has ever bought a house has looked at that first payment and wondered, "how am I going to do this for 30 years?" But, in a very short time that monthly payment has become a natural and expected item which we meet with ease. Down the line most of us wonder what the big deal was in the first place. This is simply another example of how we change our thinking. Think it will be done, Creative Force mirrors that thought and guess what, it is done!

Now let's move into the third example about picturing it: a project is coming up at work we would rather not be part of. We have placed the demand into Creative Force and it automatically responds with "you got it; you are not on this project". The interesting part just got more interesting.

We as physical/creative beings have at our disposal a limited number of options to get out of that project: 1) someone else gets the assignment 2) the project is cancelled 3) you get a different assignment. But Creative Force has these options, and an unlimited number of others. It is not bound by our range of possibilities, It may respond to our demand to be free of this project by a) having the job cancelled b) your company goes out of business c) you being fired d) the job changing to one you want to be involved with e) you break your leg and are laid up until the job is completed, and right through to z and beyond. You see how it works? Place a demand (even if it is from limited thinking), Creative Force always responds from unlimited.

It's true; even that broken leg which sidelines you can be the direct YES response of Creative Force answering your demand. Remember, Creative Force does not filter, judge or otherwise manipulate your demand; It simply mirrors what you expect from all that is possible.

This brings us to the actual creative thought and why it is so important that we are conscious of our thinking process. Every demand we place which is backed by the full power of our personal thought produces results. Be conscious of your thoughts; be conscious of what you want to experience. This does not imply you must micro-manage Creative Force, we are simply not capable of that; that's above our pay grade. What we can do as our part of the process (thinking), is to be clear in our demands on Creative Force. If I do not want to be involved in a particular project, rather than blurting out "I don't want that", shift your thinking around to saying "I am only involved in projects which fill me with joy, projects that are life affirming and bring me in contact with others who are of the same level, or higher level, of awareness." Now we have opened the door to a whole range of possibility. We have opened the door to being involved in projects which are joy filled and rewarding. If it turns out we are indeed assigned to work on the project we thought we wanted out of, it is because that assignment is in accordance with our demands on Creative Force.

Whatever demands we place into Creative Force: things, experiences, money, relationships, to realize these demands in our lives clearly we must first be clear in our own thought about what we want. How it is delivered is not our business that's why we must remember: the clearer the thought, the clearer the demonstration, the easier it is to see the gift as it arrives.

I think clearly about what I want, then allow Creative
Force to deliver it to me perfectly every time.

Fear

Oh, that four letter F word: fear. In the history of humankind no other four letter word has blocked off our good so quickly. Fear has been the clarion call for armies to march, sent to war by those who feared the other side would get the upper hand over them. Fear sets into motion what some have called the two basic instincts of humans: fight or flight. Fear extinguishes hope faster than anything else. Fear crushes the individual spirit more effectively than reality ever could.

What is fear? I have heard fear defined as 'false expectations appearing real', but my personal definition is: **F**inding **E**xcuses **A**nd **R**estraints. Fear is so powerful because just as with Creative Force, it is not constrained by "reality." Fear is not constrained by truth. Fear has free reign in our thoughts, but only to the degree we allow. Fear grows in the nutrient rich soil of our own creative thinking, but fear has no such nutrient in Creative Force, so when we hear the sound of fear in our lives, one thing is certain; we are not hearing Creative Force speaking to us.

Realizing what fear is, is important in the Think, Believe, Receive process because our thoughts set Creative Force in motion. Creative Force happily responds with a mirror image of our thoughts, this is why when we *think* fear, we get fear. The more fear we think, the more we have to fear until there is little place in our own creative beings for anything except fear. Once fear takes over our minds, there is hardly room for anything else, but there is still a little room and through our *thinking* we can reverse this trend so that with that shift in how we think, there will be little room for fear.

We may say what we want is a satisfying relationship yet we refrain from experiencing that very relationship because we FEAR we might get hurt. We are Finding Excuses (possible hurt) for not allowing the perfect relationship into our experience; we actually restrain ourselves, and our joy. As we live in fear of being hurt, sending out thoughts of being hurt, Creative Force hears from us "prove my expectation that I will get hurt" by arranging the perfect match for that experience. (Remember the mirror?) Living in fear of any experience sets up the very experiences which fulfill our expectations. What we expect to experience demonstrates itself in our lives every time.

This is where we can change how we *think* to produce a life free of fear. As we stop Finding Excuses And Restrictions in our lives we open the door to that perfect relationship, abundance, joy, perfect health, whatever it is we seek.

When we fear doing anything because of what might happen we have removed ourselves from the only place we have any power—the now because we are living in a future which may or may not come to pass. (See chapter 4 Now, Now, Now). What we are doing is shouldering aside Creative Force, which is unlimited, and replacing It with our limited thinking. We are choosing limited thinking over unlimited possibility. Does that make any sense to you?

Three steps: Think, Believe, Receive. Begin by tailoring your *Thinking* to the now. Stop Finding Excuses And Restrictions; place yourself on the side of possible. Trust that as you do this the Unlimited will fill that space that was filled with fear and provide the fulfilling relationship you seek, open the door to a better job, and unleash the creativity to write or paint or build. Creative Force cannot deliver possibility to a space that is already filled with fear, but as your thinking changes, fear will shrink, creating space and possibility will flow in to fill that void.

Just as we have already done in several instances, when fear pops up, break it into smaller pieces; pieces which can be resolved through the correct use of thinking. Let's walk through an example. Let's say your demand on Creative force is "I want a satisfying relationship".

Ask yourself:

1) What am I afraid of?

    Answer: I am afraid I might get hurt.

2) If I get hurt what would be the result?

    Answer: I would be more fearful to try again.

3) Is this hurt life threatening or does it cause harm to another?

    Answer: No, it would be emotional pain only.

4) Could I find something in this experience which would help me grow?

    Answer: Yes, I would be more aware of what I *don't* want.

5) Could I re-phrase this event into a positive experience?

    Answer: Yes, I would be more aware of what I *do* want.

6) Now that I realize this, am I at the mercy of others? Am I a victim?

    Answer: No, I am at choice in creating my perfect relationship.

Through this process we have moved from excuses and restraints (living out of our place of power in the maybe future) to our place of power in the now, the place of choice, the place of self empowerment.

Each case is unique, each question is personal, yet the process is constant.

1) Identify the fear you want to change.

2) Walk through these steps until the fear has a face and a name.

3) Realize that you have drawn the face and given it a name.

4) Because you have drawn the face and given it a name, you can re-draw the face and re-name your relationship to it.

5) Define steps you might take to avoid the same experience again by finding a positive statement about the experience. In doing this you get back to your place of power, the place from which you can move forward.

Fear has power over us only because it is nameless and formless. Right here and now give yourself permission to eliminate fear's creative hold on you and bring to bear the power of Creative Force within you, and then create possibilities to move forward in Joy.

I am unlimited. I release excuses and restraints, to
accept positive reasons and possibility in my life.

Affirmations

Each of these discussions concludes with an affirmation intended to bolster the unlimited creative power you already have within you and use every day. However, unto themselves, affirmations are useless, and sometimes even counter-productive.

I recall working for a real estate agent, Joan. Joan had spent thousands of dollars to attend a seminar designed to increase her sales. Follow-up telephone consultation was charged in the hundreds of dollars. The point here is that Joan had literarily invested heavily in trying to reach new heights of success. Each time she telephoned her real estate 'guru' Joan would receive a new affirmation. Throughout her home, on mirrors, doors, on the dresser, in the kitchen, were affirmations: "I am a persuasive salesperson. I am successful", that type of thing. Each affirmation was a great thought, to be sure, yet Joan's sales remained in the dumpster. It was like she couldn't sell a parka to a freezing man!

Does this mean Joan was simply a terrible sales person who should consider a new career? Does it show affirmations are useless? Hardly. The reason these wonderful affirmations were not producing financial results was where Joan was in her thinking process.

Joan was trying to find her power through the force of her personal will. She was trying to power the Unlimited herself, and not one of us has that much energy. Her thinking process was "If I say these words with enough feeling, say them loud enough and often enough I will sell lots and lots of houses". But saying the words is only part of the affirmation process. Joan was unaware of the Creative Force behind all thought and affirmations. The true power of affirmations does not reside in our thought alone, it does not reside in the volume or intensity with which we repeat our affirmations, the true power of affirmations resides and manifests to the extent we unite the creative power of our thought and word with Creative Force. Then and only then does the full positive result of affirmations become manifest.

Do you recall our discussion about balance? How our true nature, the full manifestation of our human selves, comes about only when both aspects of our being: physical and Creative Source come into alignment? Affirmations, prayers, meditation, contemplation are wonderful tools if we allow ourselves to stop "efforting" which means stop trying to make results happen by ourselves.

Unto themselves, no matter how cleverly written or catchy they may be, affirmations do not produce results from our thought alone. The power of affirmations rests and has its being in the co-creation of our personal minds, and Creative Force. Then and only then is the power circle completed.

Affirmations set up in our minds a clear thought, such as 'I am a great salesperson'. Once uttered, (and the more frequently the better until the desired results are demonstrated) the real power of affirmation begins to do its work to the extent we allow Creative Force to come into our being. We must allow both aspects of the e creative process, the physical and spiritual, to come into play to realize the full power of affirmations.

If you have a favorite affirmation, an affirmation about something you really want to see manifest in your life, and until now this has not seemed to have happened, take a step back: ask yourself "is this affirmation reflecting what I truly seek? Am I trying to effort this thing or experience into manifestation or am I using it as a gateway to my full power?"

Any affirmation we created in Think, Believe, Receive may be totally useless to you because it comes from our perspective. Your perspective is unique and perfect in itself, so don't hesitate to alter the affirmations you find in this book to suit your perfect desire.

Affirmations are gateways to the Unlimited, a reminder to ourselves that we open the gate in our own way; it is after all our gate! If you don't feel the power *behind* the words, they are just words. Find the feeling, and most importantly, find your connection to Creative Force as you speak your affirmation. I recognize when I have found the right affirmation for a situation because I get goose bumps as I repeat the phrase. Sometimes my lips broaden into a smile I don't want to hide. This tells me that not only have I found the perfect words, but that those words are powered by more than my vocal chords; those words are co-powered by Creative Force.

I have written thousands of affirmations for myself and others over the years, but I will let you in on a little secret: I have never found a more powerful affirmation, a more focused feeling from any combination of phrases and words than I have found in two simple words. I AM. With those two words I connect with Creative Force immediately. I allow those two words to reverberate throughout my being until a joyful feeling flows through my whole body, and then I know Creative Force and I are in perfect alignment. No other words are necessary because I have ceased efforting and allowed the power of Creative Force to flow through me.

Try it. Put this book down, sit comfortably, close your eyes and say, I AM, then listen, feel, allow. Let the phrase I AM be your only thought, and enjoy the power!

I AM. All that is, I AM

Check List for Think

How am I thinking?

1) Am I acting or re-acting to this situation? Am I living in my own power or am I living in the past?

2) Do I accept responsibility for my actions where I can change things? Or am I running for cover behind someone else?

3) In everything I do or say, am I conscious of the Law of Cause and effect?

4) Am I living in my power, in the Now, Now, Now?

5) Does what I am doing or saying come from balance, a combination of the personal me and Creative Force?

6) Do I have a clear picture of what I think I want?

7) Have I released my faith in fear?

8) What am I affirming? Am I efforting, or allowing my full power to manifest?

BELIEVE

Every time you state what you want or believe, you're the first to hear it. It's a message to both you and others what you think is possible. Don't put a ceiling on yourself.
(Oprah Winfrey)

Men often become what they believe themselves to be. If I believe I cannot do something, it makes me incapable of doing it. But when I believe I can, then I acquire the ability to do it even if I didn't have it in the beginning.
(Mahatma Gandhi)

In the sky, there is no distinction of east and west: people create distinctions out of their own minds and then believe them to be true.
(Prince Gautama Siddharta, the Buddha)

To believe is to take the first step to accomplishment.
(Brian Graham)

Where's my Power?

In the *Think* chapter of this book we discussed where our power is. As you recall, our power is in the Now, Now, Now. Our power cannot be in the past, the past is already written, and our power cannot be in the future, those pages aren't even in the book yet. That leaves the only place of our power in the Now.

Where we are in the Now is shaped by our belief. If our *belief* is that all this self empowerment stuff is pure hokum designed to separate us from our hard earned dollars, our now, our place of power, is governed and is demonstrated as a result of that *belief*. If our *belief* now is that we are unworthy of more money than we can spend, that is our reality. If our *belief* is that all the good men (or women) are taken, Creative Force affirms this for us. If we *believe* we are destined to live our lives getting-by paycheck to paycheck, that is our *belief*, our truth and that is what we are experiencing.

What we experience is totally governed by what we believe. "But wait!" you say, "I learned seeing is believing!" Well, dear friend, that is backwards. It is one of the falsehoods of our experience as physical beings.

A few years ago I had the pleasure of sitting in a plush booth at a casino theatre in Las Vegas. The lights went down, the curtain raised and there before my eyes were Siegfried and Roy along with a number of beautiful men and women. So far what I saw I believed. Out came a huge metal cage containing a magnificent white tiger. I saw it, and I believed it. A curtain was draped over the cage and moments later as the curtain was removed I saw that the tiger was gone and there sat Roy in the same place the tiger had been in the cage. Now, I saw it all with my own eyes, so am I locked into what I have been taught that seeing is believing? Did the tiger change into Roy? Did the tiger somehow become a non-form? I saw it, must I believe it? Over the course of the next two hours I saw tigers disappear, a girl sawn in half (her arms and legs wiggled after she was cut in half!) I saw people fly, an elephant vanish before my eyes; because I saw it must I believe it? Heck no. This was wonderful, beautiful and skillfully staged illusion. I, as the ticket purchaser agreed to be part of these illusions for my own entertainment. I could just as easily have sat there in disbelief saying, "there is a trap door, there is a false bottom, there is a curtain and mirrors, there are two girls in that box", whatever I thought would explain away what I had seen. Tigers don't vanish, people don't fly unassisted. If someone runs a saw through a woman what they would experience is a murder investigation and a long stay in prison, (or something more drastic). But I agreed to accept the illusion that somehow the physical laws I know were for some reason suspended for the two hours I was in the Mirage theatre in Las Vegas.

Our physical lives are much like these wonderful, amusing and even breathtaking illusions. They are presented for our entertainment. We purchase a ticket to this physical reality and in doing so we agree to suspend what our eternal beings know while we are here in favor of maybe 100 years of entertainment. But somewhere along the line we begin to believe that what is simply illusion is reality. For instance, we are taught and agree to accept that this book is solid. The reality is that this book is not solid at all. It is comprised of an uncountable number of particles of energy and each of these forms of energy has space between them, so where is the solid? The solid concept lives in our belief, in our agreement to see things a certain way.

We are taught that we exist only as long as we have physical life. When we "die" (another illusion we sometimes agree to accept) we cease to exist. Perhaps your teaching suggests we will go to a heaven and walk around golden streets with harps and angels wings. Maybe you have been taught you will return in a different body to live again. These are your personal beliefs. I will not in any way belittle your beliefs; they are yours and that is that. Still, for every given belief there are countless variations, all valid to the holder of that belief. Nothing I can say or do will sway you from your belief, until and unless you agree. Now that is true personal power! Let me say that again; nothing I can say or do, and by extension, nothing anyone else says or does, can sway you from your belief, unless and until you agree to be swayed.

Why is this concept so important to the creative process of Think, Believe, Receive? How does the description of Siegfried and Roy's magic act fit into the creative process of Think, Believe, Receive? Simply because this world is an illusion we have all agreed to share, and because the choice to accept that belief was and is yours. You and you alone can and do alter that belief anytime you choose. That's what we mean when we ask "Where is my power?" The answer is: in your belief!

If we choose to believe in lack and limitations, Creative Force is happy to go along with us. If we choose to believe what we have been taught about our lack of personal creative power, Creative Force is right there by our side affirming our pre-conceived notions. But when we are ready to broaden our awareness, really open our minds to the understanding that believing is seeing, well then we open ourselves to being the creative, fulfilled people we were created to be.

When we align ourselves with this awareness we step into the answer to our question: where is my power? We strip away the limitations of seeing is believing to broaden our appreciation of creating our own experience in concert with the unlimited Creative Force. We partner-up with the All There Is. We have already been using this power, in many cases to affirm our limitation, now let's consciously use it to empower ourselves. After all, believing IS seeing!

I choose to see and live the unlimited possibility of my being.

The Law of Attraction in my Life

The Law of Attraction is one of the Universal Laws at work in our lives each and every moment. The Law of Attraction begins with our beliefs. Let's say it has been your experience that every man you have known is selfish and self-centered. You have case history after case history to prove this thesis. The stories you tell your friends are filled with detail of the thoughtless actions of the men you have dated, and every story about these experiences is met by your listeners with the same story, or an even more hair-raising, stomach churning story. The more stories you hear which validate this belief, the more you believe your position. Enter the Law of Attraction. Because your belief is that all men are selfish and self centered, what you are sending out to Creative Force and Its Creative Medium, is the request to send you more men who fit this profile. Creative Force only hears your belief and mirrors that belief right back. Creative Force does not judge your belief, Creative Force does not say, 'let's give her another type of man so she can see she is wrong', or 'we see she is hurting so we will ignore her belief and send Mr. Right'. Creative Medium only acts upon your belief, so guess what comes into your experience time after time: Mr. Wrong and you get to be right again and again. Creative Force only agrees with our beliefs and mirrors those beliefs back into our lives with experiences which support our notions. We create and then attract these experiences.

Now, just for a moment lets say you change your thinking just a little bit. For just a moment you begin to believe it is still possible to find a man (or woman) who is kind, considerate and supportive. Now you are sending out to Creative Force a different type of message, the possibility of an experience with happy ending. You have opened the door to the possibility that the next encounter could be Mr. Right. This remains true as long as you remain open to that possible experience, but if the old belief is still active, the very first time he does something that looks like selfishness, bang, the door shuts and you validate your old belief system again and you are right back where you started. The irony here is that you get to be right again, and unhappy, again.

The creative process of Think, Believe, Receive depends upon a profound change in how you think and what you believe. Throughout your life you have changed your beliefs as your world expanded. This is your next opportunity to make a change again, especially where those old beliefs have resulted in the kinds of experiences you no longer want in your life.

What we are attempting to do here is gently release you from the established belief that what your life has been until now; how you have thought until now, must continue to be your experience. So often we want to make a change but are reluctant to do so because it means letting go of the familiarity of the old belief systems. As unfulfilling as they may be, as painful as they may be, we still cling to those belief patterns because they are familiar. Creative Force does not keep us limited to what we have done and thought before this moment. We are not condemned to continue to experience less than the best in our lives because until now we have believed a certain way. The Law of Attraction is our servant, not our master. It will deliver to us ANYTHING we believe we can have. If you continue to believe only "bad" relationships will come into your life, the Law of Attraction will provide that experience. When you shift your beliefs to the idea that you are worthy of a loving, satisfying relationship what you begin to send out is the message 'I Am Worthy of a satisfying relationship', and the Law of Attraction will just as readily respond to your new belief, and provide you with that relationship.

Until now your thought process has been one way, so let's walk through this new way of thinking:

A) Write down something you want in your life.

(*I want a satisfying relationship which is filled with fun*)

B) List as many desired details about that something as you can.

(*Supportive of my dreams, willing to listen, emotionally available*)

C) Write down the beliefs you had about this idea.

(*All men are pigs, selfish*)

D) List specific examples of experiences which
do not support this old belief.

(*Phillip and Aaron had good points, they were not selfish*)

E) How could I change my thinking to allow these traits into my life?

(*I will look for more positive traits in the people I meet*)

F) State your new belief, the one you want Law
of Attraction to hear and act upon.

(*I am fully open to attracting someone who fulfills the desires I
listed(in step B) and then to recognizing them when they arrive.*)

What you create in the final step now becomes your personal affirmation for your new experience to the degree you believe you can achieve it. This is not an exercise you do once and forget. For every topic you want to improve, refinement of your belief will be necessary. Every clarification you make redefines your belief. Your new belief is broadcast to the law of Attraction and will manifest in your life. Period.

The Law of Attraction is your servant, so get it working to produce what you want in your life.

Simply stated: the Law of Attraction means "Like is drawn unto itself".

If you want a loving relationship you must first believe a loving relationship in your life is possible, and secondly, act according to what you want in your life. You may have heard the phrase "Be the change you want to see". This simply means you yourself must live the qualities you seek in another. Remember like attracts like.

The Law of Attraction and I now work together
to create perfect results in my life.

Creative Constipation

Colorful phrase, isn't it—Creative Constipation? Yet we all too often experience this phenomenon on our path to conscious use of Think, Believe, Receive. We find it difficult to believe the unlimited power of the universe is truly on our side and when we become aware it is indeed on our side it can seem overwhelming in its scope, so powerful and filling we don't necessarily know how to use it all, thus Creative Constipation, which is also known as confusion.

Creative Force is our co-creator every moment of every day, but it is impossible to create health, prosperity, loving relationship or joy in our lives when we do not have a clear concept of what exactly we want to create or how to get there.

Let's begin with the premise that if we can conceive it, we can achieve it. This is limitlessness in action. There are an unlimited number of options we can act upon at any given moment but in order to accept these options we must first have them in our own belief system clearly. Creative Force is always going to say yes, always going to get on board with our dreams, this is a given and the basis of our premise that if we can conceive it, we can achieve it.

No projects, this book included, would ever come into being if once conceived and actually begun, with the inspiration flowing (which is

Creative Force in action supplying our demand!) and then we give up. We give up because in its perfection, Creative Force can actually overload us if we are not prepared to accept the bounty It provides. Ideas begin to pile up; so many leads and possible directions seem to sprout from the very inspiration we sought that they can begin to merge and even become overwhelming. The challenge at this point is how to sort through all these inspirations and bring your project into being. This is where so many great ideas wither and die on the vine, and this is what we refer to as Creative Constipation. So many good ideas flowing too rapidly to proceed. Remember, Creative Force does not know pacing or time at all. Ask and it is delivered. Ironically, this massive of download of creative possibility is the result of you having been clear in your demands on Creative Force. Because when we are clear in what we want, Creative Force can clearly connect us with an unlimited number of possibilities from which to choose. This is not the time to loose the focus which produced this fantastic idea response. We must believe we can handle the delivery and accept this unlimited possibility into our lives. And here is some good news: right along with these abundant ideas, Creative Force also delivers a tutorial for putting it all together, if we listen. The belief that we can find the way to incorporate all this input in a cohesive manner will lead the way to finding this tutorial.

Discovering where this tutorial is to be found may begin with a period of quiet contemplation or meditation. It may help to keep in mind that we would not be deluged with so many wonderful ideas if the best possible manner in which to implement them was not also present. Believe that because these ideas are flowing, the guidance is present as well. One never scales a mountain at one leap. One climbs the mountain one step at a time. Even with this tutorial it is easy to loose our way if we attempt to 'effort' our way through the project. Divine ways are different than physical ways. Allow yourself to be guided through the entire project from a spiritual prospective. Try an outline format. Write it out. Go back and forth between the pages of ideas always listening for your guidance. Then flesh out these outline ideas with more complete thoughts. Even as these complete thoughts come into being, remain open to the guidance which brought you this far, Creative Force will never fail you. If at some point you find you must re-do a whole section of the project, understand it was not a lacking on the part of Creative Force, or on your part, but as part of the process; perhaps you had to get to a certain point, then back-track to fully comprehend the perfect final form as Creative Force would have it. Always come back to knowing you are divinely guided in all you do to the extent you permit and listen.

Creation can not come from chaos. The immediate response to your request may look chaotic and muddled, but to avoid creative constipation and the inclination to release the project, to let another good idea die, simply remember that the clarity you seek is already wonderfully present in the process.

Creative Force is unlimited in how It delivers our good. We as physical expressions of this Unlimited do have the capacity to process the unlimited, but it sometimes requires us to be willing to step back, to realign with Creative Force, and then begin again. Creative constipation is the result (never the cause) of our own human limitations in dealing with the Unlimited, and further, it is only our perceived limitation which results in confusion. Believe that what seems like confusion is the gift within the gift because it gives us more time to really get our minds around something wonderful.

You have placed a demand on Creative Force, it has answered with a massive download of response, and here is where our participation can begin to sort it out. Get clearly in mind what you can do to move the project forward.

1) What is it I want to create?

2) Break it down; define what each of these things will look like in your life.

3) Point-by-point further break down any areas where you feel stuck. Ask yourself what might it take to open the door?

4) Take these clarified ideas and create action steps (remember, NOW is your power).

5) Prioritize these action steps based on their importance to you: begin at the beginning, remember, be in the NOW...

6) Always keep in mind the ultimate goal of each of these steps. Creative force will continue to provide ideas and guidance all along the way, so you may have to reconfigure your action steps and priorities.

7) Always believe you are guided every step of the way to your goal.

Any Bride who has planned a wedding sooner or later 'hits the wall' of Creative Constipation; location, time, guests, flowers, officiate, dress, attendants, reception, honeymoon. This is her mountain and she successfully climbs this mountain one item, one step, at a time. The most fulfilling, happy weddings are the result of the bride and other planners keeping in mind the ultimate goal of a perfect wedding rather than fixating on the perfection of the individual steps. Once a priority has been established, she keeps in mind that the right florist will appear at the right time; the perfect location is already waiting and will reveal itself at the perfect time, that every detail she has outlined for herself is also outlined for Creative Force to arrange perfectly, as she allows.

Regardless of the name of your project, the number of dollars involved or number of people involved. Regardless of the seeming complexity of the project, avoid the drama of Creative Constipation by working in concert with the one Source which can never be overwhelmed or confused by details. Make your second step (the first step was placing the demand into Creative Force) listening to your guidance. When it becomes necessary to write out the steps you envision, be open to guidance which may lead you to alter those steps. At every opportunity be aware you are not powering this project by yourself, you are the co-creator with Creative Force, and the result will always perfect.

Creative Constipation is supply in abundance;, abundance of possibility, abundance of love. I open myself to the perfect clarity within this supply.

Expectations

Are expectations and beliefs the same thing? Sort of. You see, beliefs lead to our expectations. Expectations are based on our established beliefs and are a result of our experience and the experience of everyone who has lived before. We have discussed this point before when we looked at how believing is seeing, still it deserves another examination in the context of this section on Belief.

If we expect to be guided and inspired every step of our respective journeys, we shall not be disappointed. This can work for us or against us. My Mother used to tell me "expect the best, but prepare for the worst." Sorry Mom, but this idea sets up in my mind the possibility of failure, perhaps even an expectation of failure. In her desire to see that I had a good life Mom once gave me a book entitled "What Color is Your Parachute?" This book was written from the concept of thinking through your career path. On the surface this does not seem like such a bad idea, but it did not take into consideration the presence of Creative Force in all our plans. At that time I was in radio— a disc jockey. Mom simply did not conceive of the possibility that spinning records and chatting between songs could sustain my future need for income. What she did not take into consideration was that those years behind a microphone would be essential in the development of a successful pulpit minister. Being a DJ was just one step in my experience which would lead to my present level of joy. Her expectation was of failure as she knew it. My belief, on the other hand, was that everything would be OK. I might not be walking a path she would have me walk, but within me I knew this was my path. Now, how did I know that? I cannot say. I had certainly not grasped the idea of the presence of Creative Force in my life even though it was manifesting through me all the time, I simply had a feeling of calm about my path, knowing I was taken care of.

This is where some expectations originate— from other peoples idea of what is best for us, and of course race consciousness, which is the sum total of every thought of every person who is living and has lived. Usually when these ideas are presented to us, they are from a place of love. If we turn other peoples beliefs into our expectations we have chosen to release our power in creating our experience, we have released our belief in our own perfect expression of Creative Force.

We simply cannot live up to others expectations. When we try, we end up resentful and dissatisfied in our own life.

This creative process called Think, Believe, Receive is our individual process. Our thinking is what sets Creative Force in action; our belief in our own worthiness to realize these goals brings them to manifestation.

Others beliefs which lead us to our expectations limit us. Our own beliefs which lead to our expectations empower us IF, and only to the extent our expectations and beliefs are based on the truth that Creative force wants us to have all we desire. Right now choose to shape your own beliefs consciously.

Here are examples of expectations and how we might find ourselves creating our own lives based around others beliefs.

Doctors say 75% of all patients with a certain symptom die from that symptom.

Is your belief that you will die or is your belief that you are in the 25% who will live joyfully?

Statistics indicate 50% of all marriages end in divorce.

Is your belief there is no use in getting married, that it will end in divorce, or is your belief that you will be among the 50% who live harmoniously and lovingly with your partner for the rest of this lifetime?

If I adhere to this religious tenant doggedly I will be happy.

Is your belief that someone else can define your happiness or is it your belief that you are always guided and loved by Creative Force regardless of your religion?

In these examples expectations are **highlighted** and underlined. Belief in these expectations can go either way, always dependant on your choice: they can help, or hinder your freedom. Your expectation surrounding each of these examples will define and shape your belief as well as your experience. Our place of power to experience the most fulfilling life rests within ourselves. Do we blindly adhere to what others believe, or do we align ourselves with the Unlimited and create our own beliefs? Either way it is we ourselves who ultimately make the choices. The "Others" who make pronouncements are not living our lives; they are not experiencing our experiences. Each of us is walking a path no other person in history has ever walked. Statistics reflect the specific experiences of human kind through someone else's perspective and interpretation. You are you and a more magnificent you has never been, and never will be. There is no reason to accept what others think you will experience as your belief.

When you set a goal, be it getting out of bed or making a billion dollars it is essential to examine your expectations and then create your own belief system around what you want. Any expectation will take root and bear fruit according to your belief, so right now, examine your expectations and see if they are yours, or if they have been given you through race consciousness. If they are yours, embrace them, empower them with the belief you are guided by Creative Force to their perfect fruition.

My expectations are powered by the possible and I believe I am unlimited in every way to their joyful manifestation.

Giving it Away

Self empowerment— realizing the Creative Force within ourselves is our goal through Think, Believe, Receive. You have diligently applied your own creative force to the exploration, definition and refinement of what you want in your life. You have done a fantastic job of visioning and clarifying your goals and defining others expectations from your own beliefs. Everything is in place for a dynamic realization of every one of your goals.

Then you give it away, and it is all for naught, back to square one.

The successful implementation of Think, Believe, Receive relies upon our own personal expression of Creative Force. This is our place of power, our workplace, if you will, yet we give that power away when we allow gossip or judgment of others to enter our workplace. The male celebrity or pseudo celebrity of the week is caught cheating on his wife. The talking-heads are yapping about this report or those photos. We hear the tapes played hourly, and then we pass these "facts" along to our friends. "That's all I'm doing", you say, "passing along what I heard". But it's not that simple. In addition to 'passing along the facts' you are inadvertently reinforcing your belief about men in general, you are affirming an expectation and belief that men can not be trusted.

And this is not gender specific. Both men and women indulge in gossip and every form of gossip is giving away your own power, then it's back to square one in your creative process. Gossip always robs us of our power, right along with complaining. Gossip and complaining are two sides of the same coin.

Will Bowen has written a wonderful book entitled "A Complaint Free World". This book clearly sets out how, by complaining and gossiping, we rob ourselves of our own power. Bowen writes: "complaining is focusing on what we don't want. It's talking about what's wrong, and what we focus our attention on expands". By participating in complaining and gossip we separate ourselves from the truth that each of us is doing the best we can at any given moment. If the celebrity de jour or the person in the next cubicle seems to be acting in a manner reflecting other than this truth, we plant the seeds of doubt about our selves. We actually plant a crop of belief that we are not doing the best we can at this moment. These seeds yield a crop of self-doubt which leads directly to giving away our own power.

One of the reasons we gossip, according to Will Bowen is that it makes us feel better about ourselves. We are saying, in essence, we are better than that other person. We are attempting to justify ourselves based upon the actions of another, but there is no power in this way of thinking.

We give it away when we compare ourselves to others. Please remember, we are all perfect creations doing the best we can at any given moment. This is why we react so strongly when we learn others are gossiping about us! We challenge the gossiper to come to us and say those things to our face, simply so we can explain or defend our actions. We know that whatever these others are speaking about we did in the best manner we could manage at that time, no matter what they think, or what we would do differently next time around.

Judgment of others is the same process. When I judge you as lacking I am saying I am better than you, but how do I know what was going on in your life at that moment? I have never walked a mile in your shoes. You see, gossip and judgment, just as gossip and complaining are two sides of the same coin.

As we judge others or gossip about others, we create a belief within ourselves that there is only one way to our common goal; which is a joyful, fulfilling life. This is simply not true. I do not require your permission to follow my path and you do not require my permission to follow your path. Both paths are about finding joy and fulfillment as best we can. Gossip and judgment are distractions, even an impediment to our goal. Rather than look within for what we might be doing to improve our lot in life, we end up spending that energy in looking for ways others can improve their lives based upon our judgment of their lives, and it simply does not work. We are giving it away. It, of course being our own creative power. Bowen offers a 21 day challenge based upon the premise that it takes 21 days to break the complaint/gossip habit and re-frame our thinking. I encourage you to accept this challenge. Leave behind the destructive urge to gossip about, or judge others. Take those 21 days and all the time beyond you need to reclaim your own power of Creative Force and channel it through the belief we are all walking our own path to joy, the best way we know how at this moment. Shut off the power drain of gossip, judgment and complaining and instead believe in the power of the conscious use your beliefs and your own self empowerment. Quit "giving it away!"

I release gossip, complaining and judgment in
favor of my own perfect unfoldment.

Gimme my Stuff

Among the many things we have been taught either indirectly by our parents and various other teachers (sometimes called race consciousness), or directly through our life experience (which in turn becomes part of race consciousness), is that to want "stuff", more money, a new car, better health, sobriety, is greedy. We have been taught that there is glory in suffering; that wanting to be more and have more is selfish; that to deprive ourselves in this life will lead to greater glory in the next is the only right way to live.

Sometimes well meaning people will challenge us with the idea that for us to want more is wrong while there are people starving all over the world, people living in cardboard boxes right in our own country. How dare we ask for more!

With love, I must draw the proverbial line in the sand and reply: rubbish!

You cannot be poor enough to help another person. You cannot live in squalor extensive enough to house another family. We are eternal beings having a physical experience, right along with those whose only food is what they can salvage from refuse containers. This is not to say we should not give to charities which help others with fewer resources than ourselves; in fact in a later chapter we will discuss the power of tithing and charity. Give. Give whatever you can, help as you are able, but there is no nobility in lack for the sake of lack. Make this your belief.

This belief in lack and the potential rewards for self-denial to be repaid at a future time runs counter to the very power of Creative Force. It is a limiting belief designed to control how we think; to enrich those who create this "moral high ground." If we find ourselves buying into this way of thinking, when we do allow prosperity into our lives we find ourselves burdened with guilt for our gains. Guilt is another disempowering belief which robs us of our innate creative force (although we have to admit, it is a great system if we are the beneficiary of that guilt). Rather than believe in guilt about having more stuff, reverse your perception and realize that you cannot experience more good without also producing more good stuff for others as well. It is impossible for us to experience more good for ourselves without increasing the available good for all

The entire idea that wanting stuff is evil is based upon the belief of limitation. If I get a raise or win the lottery, that means there is less for others. Right now, let's call in our friends, Law of Attraction and the Law of Cause and Effect (aka Karma). If I believe in lack and limitation, what will I attract? If I believe in lack and limitation, what do I experience? The Law of Attraction says I will attract proof of lack and limitation. If I believe in lack and limitation, how does The Law of Cause and Effect show up in my life? Lack and limitation. There is a perfect, consistent and undeniable relationship going on here.

Having said this, we want to refer to the previous chapter on balance. If every waking moment I am focused on getting more stuff to the exclusion of my connection to Creative Force, then we will agree; wanting stuff is indeed out of integrity. Balance in all things is essential to our well being and the creative power contained in the Think, Believe, Receive process.

No material thing alone will bring you happiness. No relationship will fill you with joy and peace of mind. No house is fancy enough to make you feel secure; no alarm system will make you feel safe. In Alcoholics Anonymous one of the teachings is if you put a jerk on a plane in Los Angeles, and fly him to New York, a jerk will get off the plane in New York. Location is not enough to find peace of mind or sobriety.

All stuff; all possessions are effect, not cause. All stuff is the end result of a process (effect) which always begins with a thought. To become more powerful, more accurate in creating your "stuff" it is essential to remember we are a part of something much larger, more powerful than our own individual beings. This power is the only true cause of all stuff.

Peace, joy, happiness, healthfulness, fulfilling relationships, physical comfort, sobriety, are the end result, the effect, of finding your place in being as a full, important, meaningful part of Creative Force. We are referring to a Spiritual Relationship, and it is ours right now to the extent we accept and believe this as our truth.

The celebrity de jour on TMZ who seems to have the world on a string; unlimited income, fame, all the stuff one could want, and still gets caught shoplifting a scarf or jailed for illegal drugs is a clear and constant reminder to us that stuff alone is never, never, never enough. There must be a Spiritual Connection to create a balance with all that stuff.

When we isolate ourselves from the whole spectrum of life to concentrate solely on private jets, exclusive party rooms and 'peeps' who reflect back to us only the value of stuff, we isolate ourselves from the Spiritual Truth which is the real Cause. The end results are often tragic. You see, human kind was never intended to define itself as a bunch of individuals completely apart from all the other individuals and our connection to Creative Force. Yes, we are individuals, that is one of the most magnificent aspects of creation; billions and billions of individuals, all with their own view of life, and yet we all have a common connection: a connection to Creative Force. We are part of a fabric, part of an interwoven system which gives meaning to our very being. If we view ourselves as existing for only 60, 70, maybe 100 years and then that's it, there is not much motivation to seek happiness, what would be the point?

Every aspect of Think, Believe, Receive is based upon the truth that we are eternal beings, spiritual beings, having a physical experience. From this place of belief we are not alone, even for an instant. We have placed ourselves in the position of experiencing everything for the first time, as we have said, no one has ever walked your path before, and still we are part of this interwoven fabric of the Cosmos. What a wonderful support system. If this were not the truth, how could prayer be answered? If this was not the truth, how could intuition work, how could Creative Force conspire to respond affirmatively to your every desire?

There is nothing wrong in wanting more and better stuff or experiences. There is nothing wrong in wanting more income, perfect health or anything else; in balance.

Creative Force knows nothing of lack or limitation, both are constructs of humankind demonstrated in our physical experience through the Law of Cause and Effect and the Law of Attraction. There is nothing noble about living without what you want, so where do you place your belief: in abundance or lack?

The choices are yours, and if you find your choices do not fill you with joy, you will have another chance later to make another choice. Abundance applies to choices as well as stuff, so rest easy.

I place my belief in abundance, knowing my stuff is the direct result of Creative Force operating though my life.

Spirituality or Religion?

Our beliefs are created in large part by the influence of religion. For the person in Fargo, North Dakota the personal belief system is far different from the person in Jakarta, Indonesia mostly because of religious influence, not because, at root they want different things. You do not have to be part of any particular religion to have your belief shaped by religion; the dominant belief system of a given country is shaped by Race Consciousness which is the result of the dominant religious concept. Here in the United States we know this to be primarily a Christian influence, but that word Christian is so multi-faceted as to be almost meaningless. Baptists consider themselves to be Christians, so do Catholics, but their practices are miles apart! Mormons consider themselves to be Christians but their teachings have little in common with Lutherans, who also consider themselves Christians.

Every major religion has a version of the afterlife and the Supreme Being— why then have we waged war in the name of God since the beginning of time? The short answer must be: Religion.

The people of India lived for thousands of years in cooperative peace between Muslims and Hindus until one day fear raised its ugly head. Muslims who had lived in peace with Hindi, who shared food, work; even in some cases inter-married with each other suddenly feared their neighbors simply because of the others religion. The resultant chaos took form in the creation of an entire country: Pakistan, where Muslims felt they could live in peace with their religion and Hindis could live in peace in India with their religion. It didn't work out that way, did it? India and Pakistan now stand poised to obliterate themselves, each other and a good portion of the earth with atomic weapons pointed at each other, all in the name of religion.

From this perspective the indictment against religion is quite compelling, religion must be bad. Religion causes war, religion kills people, but here again, if we take this stand we find ourselves out of integrity, out of balance. Religion itself is not bad, nor is it good, until the people who practice that religion act or re-act in the name of that religion.

At the core of all actions are people: individuals like you and me. Beauty, love, truth is found in every religion yet the individuals who act in its name often forget the very spirituality which was the founding premise of that religion and act far outside it original intent. How can a Christian ignore the commandment 'thou shalt not kill' then slaughter Muslims as they did during the Crusades. How can Muslims, whose Koran clearly states Jews and Christians are also people of "The Book" justify random acts of violence against their brothers? Because these acts are not committed by religions, they are committed by individuals whose beliefs have been manipulated away from the spiritual truths which are the basis of their religion.

It is not our premise that any religion is good, nor that any religion is bad, we bless them all. Our premise is we can all benefit from a little less religious dogma and a lot more spiritual belief.

Think, Believe, Receive is many things, what it is not is a religion. Regardless of your commitment to a religion or commitment from religion the concepts offered here can and do serve to enhance your spiritual experience, to raise your thoughts from a background noise to a conscious awareness of their presence in your life and create a more meaningful and fulfilling experience.

Religion, therefore, is defined as a structure of ritual, and tradition, which at some point had its origins in a Spiritual Concept. Religion grew from our need as physical beings to come to terms with our questions about why things happen: at this point religion served to feed us spiritually, to give us comfort, to help us understand our place in the grand scheme of things. Over time however, religion has grown to be its own justification. We have taken our comfort and labeled it as Methodist, Calvinist, Buddhist, Judaism, whatever, then further defined it as reformed, Conservative, new, first, second, not to enhance the spiritual content, but to separate ourselves from the other guy. Those who would become the first religious leaders did not explain the natural action of the environment from the perspective of us and them; they explained these actions as applying to everyone. Somewhere along the line people got into the "Us or Them" mode of thinking and brought their religion in as their tool. No longer was the perfect and natural operation of the environment about everyone, religion came to be used to define our separateness. The lightening which religion at one time explained as the gods being angry was now redefined as the gods being angry because "those" people don't worship as we do, so it's OK to go take their stuff, or wage war upon them.

We have noted humankind was not created to act as individuals apart from one another. We were, and are, created as part of a tapestry; to revel in the majesty of the variety of creation, and by being individuals within this tapestry, to bring texture to its very existence. We are all one at our core.

One of the leading thinkers of our age in the field of Myth brilliantly underscores the importance of myth and ritual in our spiritual experience. He writes that 'there is a dramatic comfort in a body of people expressing their belief ritualistically, sharing common myth as a means to finding oneness.' Humankind however has taken these myths and rituals to an unforeseen level and used them to justify separateness rather than oneness.

Step back from the rush to judgment here. This idea of us and them, Christian and Jew, Jew and Muslim, has been created through our belief in a separateness from our Creative Force; created from a place of fear that if 'their' practices are right, ours must be wrong. If your rituals and myths bring you to the realization of oneness, of connection to each other and the entire planet, they cannot be wrong, and if mine bring me to that same place, mine cannot be wrong either. So why experience the fear?

Belief in labels such as good and bad, right and wrong, worthy and unworthy is a religion unto it self. Our mission with Think, Believe, Receive is to embrace the diversity of thought, to embrace the ultimate power of oneness as its own end and release the limitation of "us and them".

Throughout every major teaching, of which we are aware, runs the common belief in a Supreme Power which we have been calling Creative Force. God, Allah, The Universe, Spirit, All That Is, and yes, even Chuck, is the common thread running through all creation, and all religions, one cannot even be an atheist without some type of Creative Force to deny. This is the difference between religion and spirituality: Religion in many cases has become the justification for separation of us from each other and separation from the Supreme Being or Creative Force. Spirituality was the original intent and spirituality is the on-going belief that regardless of whatever effect humankind has manifested, as a group or as individuals, all is well, and all is one.

I release my belief in separation and find my joy in the diversity of creation and knowing that all is well.

Fear, the Sequel

Think, Believe, Receive is a creative three step belief process to manifest in our lives those things we want and by the same token a three step belief process to release the unwanted in our lives. Each step is part of the next step; Think, then Believe, then Receive, but it is also a circle; Think, then Believe, then Receive, then Think, then Believe, then Receive, and so on.

One simply cannot think their good into being, or believe their good into being; we must include all three steps. Just when we believe we have gotten our thinking aligned with this process something wonderful occurs; we gain a deeper understanding of the process as it applies to our personal experience. One of the bi-products of this deeper understanding can be fear: Finding Excuses And Restraints. You see, newer and deeper understandings can be a blessing, or we can re-act to them as a threat. Threatened, our natural response is to go into defense; shut down. We fear this deeper understanding means we were wrong at our previous level of understanding, and nobody wants to be wrong!

Ask yourself, was a baby wrong when she thought crying to get food was effective? No, she was doing what she learned was effective, so when physical development offered her the opportunity to communicate with words it was a joyful event, not a finding of wrong for not earlier understanding words as communication.

When a toddler advances from the tottering stage of development to smooth, confident walking was he wrong because he did not use these skills previously? Not at all.

Our own belief development reflects the same progression. We read a book such as Think, Believe, Receive and now find the Laws we have been using unconsciously have names and predictable results which are enhanced by using those same Laws consciously. The baby was using her voice to cry; now she uses that voice to talk. The toddler uses his same legs to wobble as he uses to confidently walk from room to room; no wrong, no fear. You see, becoming aware of the natural Laws of the universe and how they work in your life does not mean you were wrong before you became aware of those Laws.

Sometimes we get into fear about our own expanding belief system because we have come to equate a different level of belief with the idea that we were wrong in our previous way of belief. Fear is not our true friend. Fear can be a motivator to change, that is true, but fear can become our excuse for restraint from accepting our own expanding Spiritual aspects and possibilities.

Each moment of your life, both physical and eternal, you are growing, expanding, coming to new awareness of the majesty which is creation. We cannot move from step one to step two successfully until we have fully embraced what step one is all about, so what is the big deal about fear? When we allow fear (which again, is Finding Excuses And Restraints) to prevent us from moving into step two, or step three or step one billion six hundred three. We create as our belief that step one is all that is safe and good, and the only place we can be safe and good.

Please know with us, Creative Force wants you to be joyful in all ways. Creative Force is absent of lack and limitation, free of pain or doubt. Creative Force—the motivating energy behind everyone and everything is comprised of not only of love for you, but love of you. Creative Force cannot make you expand spiritually, but Creative Force is Omniscience, Omnipotent, and Omnipresent: all knowing, all powerful, always present to support you as it provides the opportunity for you to embrace your deepening spirituality and expand your belief system.

Fully understanding the unlimited nature of Creative Force and the manner in which it can fulfill all our desires and demands is like attempting to truly comprehend the concept of infinity. As physical beings we have a finite view of everything, including infinity and the eternal. We have no need in this physical expression of Creative Force to truly grasp what is unlimited. We need only accept, to believe the possibility. You might say understanding infinity and eternal is above our pay grade. This is why fear of an expanding awareness has no place in our development of our personal spirituality.

If you were raised Catholic and now find yourself seeking a deeper understanding of your spiritual nature, you don't have to fear your newfound expansion makes you wrong to have been brought up Catholic and you need not fear those who remain practicing Catholics or think they are wrong. Just as the baby learned to talk and the toddler learned to walk there is no wrong "back there". Creative Force has answered your demand for an expanded understanding as to how this life works, that's all. It does not even mean you cannot continue to enjoy the Catholic community. The Law of Attraction, which is an active and fully owned subsidiary of Creative Force, is at work, as you believe.

Fear can stomp out our expanding belief system more easily than Smokey Bear can stomp out a forgotten campfire, and neither fear, nor Smokey Bear is anything more than a belief system.

As Creative Force moves in your life, at your request, to expand your belief system in the loving, supportive oneness of all; recognize the re-action of Finding Excuses And Reasons to resist that expansion. You are loved, supported, guided and supplied by a Source which knows no bounds, no excuses, and no limitations.

Ask yourself: is my belief in limitation and lack or do I believe in possible?

Right now I release my belief in fear and dedicate myself to embracing unlimited possibility.

Faith

Faith is *"the substance of things hoped for, the evidence of things not seen"*, or you may be more comfortable with *"faith is the assurance of things hoped for, the conviction of things not seen"*. Either way faith means a belief in the presence of an invisible Principle and Law which directly and specifically responds to us. The difference in language between these two Biblical quotes used here is due to differences in the translation from the original text to modern usage rather than the message each contains.

We all have faith. For some of us it is faith **_in_** something, for some of us it is faith **_of_** something. This seemingly minor distinction is perhaps the most important aspect yet in our section on Belief in Think, Believe, Receive.

Faith **_in_** means we believe something can do for us. Faith **_of_** reflects a belief that the something that can do for us is part of our own being. We have discussed at length the power each of us has in our creativeness, our innate ability to create conditions. Embracing this concept requires us to be aware that our creative power is part of something much larger. We do not, by ourselves, create anything. What actually does the creating is us AND Creative Force, and we are part of Creative Force, we have faith **_of_** Creative Force. If we were to

73

attempt to demonstrate our creative ability based solely upon our own abilities all we would have to show for our efforts are wishful thinking and dreams. We demonstrate or manifest our demands only in concert with Creative Force.

The first paragraphs in this section are both Biblical quotes taken from two versions of the Bible. Regardless of the translation or your individual take on the Bible let's look at this definition and see how it fits into our discussion about belief in the creative process we call Think, Believe, Receive. "The substance of things hoped for" relates directly to our process. We want to see something particular in our lives, be it health, peace, sobriety, fulfilling relationships, whatever form we are discussing. We place into consciousness this form, and we do so as clearly as possible. That is the demand, or the "substance". We then rely upon Creative Force, which is clearly represented as "the evidence" (or conviction) of things not seen to produce the results. None of us has ever seen Creative Force. There is nothing to be seen, Creative Force simply is. None of us has seen what makes an apple seed sprout, grow into a tree and yield more apples, have we? We simply have faith that whatever powers this process will do what it does. Creative Force, powerful as it is, cannot grow an apple tree from an orange seed.

Many times in Think, Believe, Receive we have suggested the idea of Creative Force producing a mirror image of what we demand or of our thoughts. Just as Creative Force will not produce an apple tree from an orange seed, Creative Force will not produce a tree of abundance from a seed of lack, it is simply not possible.

We must have faith Creative Force will produce what we plant. This is our belief. If our belief is that Creative Force cannot produce or will not produce for us, Creative Force affirms our belief by not producing for us!   If our belief includes the affirmation "I believe I am part of Creative Force", our word or demand takes on the power

74

of the unlimited as it works through us. Conversely, if our belief is that we are separate from Creative Force, we place ourselves apart from that Force and rather than being powerful co-creators, we become powerless supplicants hoping Creative Force will respond to our pleas. The result of placing ourselves outside, seeing ourselves as apart from Creative Force is that we now have a belief in a Force which is capricious, moody and selective, yet biblical tradition aptly points out that rain falls upon the just and unjust equally. Creative Force could never choose to grow an apple tree from an apple seed for one planter and not another simply because this planter is of one religion and that planter is of another religion, or an atheist, in Creative Force we are all worthy. This is an issue of faith which is demonstrated with such perfect regularity, scientifically, we do not think of it as faith at all. But, it's still faith. We all have faith, the question is: of what do we have faith? Do we have faith in a Creative Force that may or may not cooperate in the manifestation of our desires, or do we have faith of Creative Force which works with us all the time, in every case?

You see, the demonstration (or proof if you wish) that Creative Force is always working through us is proven in the Law of Cause and Effect and the Law of Attraction. Both of these Laws we have seen proven in our lives time and again, even if we were not necessarily conscious of what that proof was at the time. The rain falls on the conscious and unconscious equally because Creative Force works through us all the time. What we seek to do through this creative process of Think, Believe, Receive is to move us into a more conscious application of these laws to create ever more powerful manifestations through the use of these Laws.

Another aspect of faith in common usage today is Karma. Unfortunately the concept of Karma has largely been usurped by a connotation of the negative. The original concept of Karma is neither positive nor negative and Karma is certainly not capricious. Today we may hear someone say "doing harm to another is bad Karma" meaning something bad will happen to us if we harm another. In the original context doing harm to another results in us experiencing something similar in this, or another lifetime. This gives us a chance to atone for the action, to do the right thing next time. In no way should we view this as negative. The truth is we cannot do harm to another without doing harm to ourselves because we are all one!

Karma is simply another term for the Law of Cause and Effect. If we have a belief Creative Force will punish us for doing harm to another we also have a belief in a vengeful Creative Force, but remember, Creative Force is never vengeful, It simply mirrors what we believe and manifests in our life as we place our faith. Karma gives us the opportunity to reform our behavior, in this life or another, giving us the opportunity to truly recognize we must treat others as we wish to be treated: to love our neighbors as our selves.

Faith is often viewed as a religious concept, something based upon nothing more than hope, yet we demonstrate faith everyday regardless of our religious or spiritual concepts. When we swing our feet out of bed in the morning and place them on the floor, not one of us, even for an instant questions that gravity will result in our feet remaining on the floor. We simply have faith it will happen.

Through the use of the creative process of Think, Believe, Receive we clarify and illustrate to ourselves how Creative Force always, always, always responds to our demands in a scientific, repeatable, predictable manner, to the degree we believe. For most of us this is not a faith we always exhibit. We develop the expectation that the Laws of Cause and Effect or Attraction work in this case, but not in that case. If this were so, these would not be Laws, they would simply be accidents.

Think, Believe, Receive is a creative process. It is also the faith that our lives are part of an infallible, loving, Creative Force which is present and active in our experience all the time.

Ask yourself: where is my faith? Is my faith in lack and limitation, judgment and capriciousness, or is my faith of a oneness which wants only good for me?

I align my faith with the unlimited good of
Creative Force working in my life now.

Checklist for Believe

What are my beliefs?

1) Is my belief in the idea that seeing is believing, or have I opened myself to knowing that believing is the true first step in seeing, the first step in true power?

2) Have I awakened myself to understanding that the Laws of Attraction, and Law of Cause and Effect are always in operation in my life, and through their use I attract to myself the experiences and things I desire?

3) Do I welcome into my experience the abundance of Creative Force even when the gift seems too much because I understand this reflects the answers to my requests, and that clarity is also part of the gift?

4) Have I aligned my expectations to reflect the belief of the unlimited good of Creative Force in my life?

5) Do I keep my personal power by foregoing gossip and judgment of others?

6) Does my belief reflect the unlimited nature of the Universe as it flows through my life?

7) Have I allowed myself to shed a belief in separation from others and find the joy in diversity and spirituality?

8) Does fear still rule my life, or have I embraced Unlimited Possibility?

9) Do I have faith in, (apart from myself), or faith of, (the oneness) which is my true being?

RECEIVE

We find what we expect to find and we receive what we ask for.
(Elbert Hubbard)

No one can ask another to be healed, but he can let
himself be healed and thus offer the other what he has
received. Who can bestow upon another what he does not
have? And who can share what he denies himself?
(A Course in Miracles)

Everything comes to us that belongs to us if
we create the capacity to receive it.
(Saint Francis of Assisi)

To give is Divine; to receive gratefully is also Divine.
(Brian Graham)

Allow it in

We would love to begin this chapter on receiving by saying this is the easiest step. We would love to say that because you have done so much good work in re-aligning your thought to the possible, opening yourself to the belief that there is a Power, of which you are part, that sees in you and wants for you only the very best, that you are now ready to receive, wham, bam, thank-you. Sometimes this is the truth; that all we have to do is shift our thinking and beliefs and the receiving is automatic, but sometimes it's not.

We have discussed the idea several times that this creative process of Think, Believe, Receive is a circle, that's why sometimes we find that while we have perfectly executed the first two steps the third step drags out, or never seems to arrive; where is the justice in that? We have promised you that this power  we call Creative Force is predictable and reliable, it is mathematical in its precision, and It is. Just as we have had to go through step after step of cleaning up our thought and belief processes sometimes we must re-examine our receiving process as well. Sometimes we discover that the way in which we have re-defined how we think and believe is so drastically different from anything we have ever experienced before, that we are not prepared to truly receive what Creative Force joyously prepared to give us. We find we must re-align our receiving tools as well, and to do this we may find that we must go back to the beginning of Think, Believe, Receive to get an even clearer idea of what it is we want to receive, what it might look like, and how this new set of ideas around thinking and believing will work in our lives. Rest assured, the gift is there, as we align ourselves with the perfect delivery of the perfect thing at the perfect time.

I recall a time when I was earning a hundred dollars a week, just enough money to pay rent, buy gas and eat on a tight budget. Of course I wanted more money! One day as I stood in line at a fast food restaurant I felt a tap on my shoulder. I turned around to see a woman holding out a ten dollar bill to me. "Here, take it" she said. Now at the time, ten dollars was more than two hours pay. I had placed into consciousness a demand for more money, and certainly ten dollars fulfilled that qualification, so Creative Force had delivered to me, to me directly, clearly and unquestionably what I had sought. Did I gratefully accept this gift and bless the giver and Creative Force (and my own participation in the cycle)? No I did not. I declined the offer. Why would I do such a foolish thing? Why did I not accept this generous gift in the spirit it was intended? Fear. (Finding Excuses And Restraints) Fear of what strings might be attached, fear of seeming needy, fear of misunderstanding the offer, maybe she was just tapping me on the shoulder and happened to have the ten dollars in her hand, wouldn't I look foolish! Fear, Fear, Fear, Finding Excuses And Restraints!

At another, very much more prosperous, time in my life I was a public relations person for a national chain of restaurants. One of the stories I heard about the founder of this highly successful chain of eateries was that as a child in his home country he had been told the streets of America were paved with gold. This became his though and belief. Finally he made it to America. As he deplaned, walking up the jet-way he noticed a five dollar bill on the ground. At this point in his life this man was wearing everything he owned on his back, yet as he looked at that five dollar bill he made the decision to leave the currency on the ground because to him that five dollars was not his next meal, that five dollars was the affirmation of all he had come to think and believe, that the streets of America were indeed lined with gold, a land of untold riches. His thought process and belief system were clear, if there is a five dollar bill here, on the ground, how much more he would receive as he entered into this new life! Within a few short years his thought and belief system had manifested into his receiving more income than he could spend.

These are two examples of almost the same story; mine took place from a position of fear and resulted in my rejecting the gift I had sought, the other came from a place of affirmation of thought and belief. Two sides of the same coin or bill if you wish. Fear was my limiting factor, belief was his empowering factor.

This is why we say, even though our demand on Creative Force is clear, our belief it will manifest steadfast, at any moment that creative loop can be broken by a little bit of fear, so we must again begin our process of Think, Believe, Receive to insure our channel of good is open, free of obstruction, ready to receive what Creative Force has already approved. In both cases the manifestation of what each of us sought was present. This is a reminder that we must participate in the demonstration to receive our good.

I keep myself aware to the fulfillment of my requests and
allow them into my life with joy and gratitude.

The Law of Correspondence

The Law of Correspondence is not unlike sending and receiving mail. If you are looking to get a letter from someone you might want to have a mailbox so the post office can deliver the letter to you. Creative Force has already approved what you want, in fact every aspect of the Universe has conspired to send you your good (the letter), and the question is: do you have a mailbox to receive the letter (your request)? To receive something you must have a corresponding space to receive. The larger you want, the larger you must be prepared to receive.

Now, let's let go of the idea that Creative Force knows anything about big or little, It simply doesn't; for Creative Force there is no size at all. Creative Force does not know the difference between one thousand dollars and one million dollars. Creative Force cares not if you desire a five year old Corolla or a brand new Ferrari; it's all the same, both are simply forms of energy. But for you and me on this physical plane there is scale, so you must create the space which is to scale with your request. That is the Law of Correspondence in our lives.

Our thought process around the idea of this Law of Correspondence is to visualize a basket. Unlike Creative Force, we do know the difference between a thousand and a million dollars, but as we await the perfect delivery of whichever sum we have requested, it is our work to insure we have created a large enough basket to accept the delivery of our demand. Perhaps we can envision ourselves getting a thousand dollars, but can we truly envision ourselves getting a million dollars? Until we create the basket large enough to accept that million, it cannot be delivered, that is the Law of Correspondence in action.

As a teenager I worked at a well known Southern California theme park. Being in high school my financial needs were modest so the $1.65 per hour I was being paid seemed a princely sum. It was enough to buy a used car, pay for the gas, and go on dates; I could even save a few dollars. That was the size of my basket, and it was filled nicely, thank you. Filling my Volkswagen gas tank cost all of $2.50. One night I borrowed my parent's car for a date. This huge Chevrolet Impala was a land yacht compared to my little bug, so when the time came to fill the gas tank during my date, imagine my consternation as the gas pump meter passed $2.50, then 5, then 10, up to $20.00! My cash reserves were essentially wiped out, there was nothing left for an after date snack. That the Impala would require more fuel, therefore more money, should not have been a surprise to me, the obvious size of the car would suggest that, but I simply had not considered this difference when planning what size basket to use for the date. I did not prepare.

Too often this is how we approach the receiving we seek. We know we want more, yet we do not create a space for that more in our lives. Our baskets are not large enough to receive what we seek. We do the right work in thinking, even align our beliefs to having those grand things in our lives, yet we block our receiving by not considering how large our basket must be to accept our bounty.

I recall a dear friend of mine, Michael, presenting a Sunday message about his plans to attend college. He placed a 12 ounce cup on the lectern and explained that Creative Force would gladly fill that 12 ounce cup if that was what he requested. Then he pulled out an 18 ounce cup to demonstrate how much he would actually need for college. Once again he explained Creative Force would just as happily fill the 18 ounce cup as the 12 ounce cup, if that was what he requested. Finally he produced a 32 ounce cup. This, he explained, would not only pay for his college, it would pay his rent, car payments and all the other expenses he would incur during his schooling. Creative Force knows no size so 16, 18, 32 ounce cup, no difference. The only difference was in what he was demanding of the Universe. When we are placing demands on Creative Force, why limit ourselves by even mulling the 16 ounce cup? Go for the 32 ounce cup, and do so by preparing yourself to truly receive that bounty. Expand your basket (or cup) to accept what the Universe will certainly provide.

It is not enough to say we want to win a 100 million dollar lottery; we must first purchase the ticket to win. We must take part in the creative process all the way through from thinking to receiving. We must then truly envision what those multi-million dollars would look like in our lives. This most certainly will include some mental housekeeping; releasing worthiness issues, for instance. If we view ourselves as unworthy to have that 100 million, how can we receive it? If you have ever said "I simply would not know what to do with that kind of money", well, that idea has to be released! To take in that 100 million dollars we have to know what we would do with that kind of money. No matter what the gift you seek in your life you must comply with the Law of Correspondence for it to arrive.

Now, here is a twist on the idea of creating space: let's say you place
 the demand for the 100 million dollar lottery prize, and you win it! Good for you, now how are you going to handle it? Unless those housekeeping chores have been done thoroughly, you will be like so many lottery winners who hit the jackpot and within a few

years are actually worse off than financially than before they won the money. Why? Because they did not have a basket large enough to accept this prize, their consciousness was not in alignment with the bounty. Without the consciousness, without complying with the Law of Correspondence, we do not get to keep the money, it flies away.

Think, Believe, Receive, then Think, Believe, Receive, and so on. Raising our consciousness to the level where we can accept all the good Creative Force has to deliver to us is an ongoing process. If the good you seek has not arrived yet, have faith, it is there. Walk the steps until you see it in your life. Oh, and go check your mailbox, maybe it has arrived!

I allow my basket to grow larger and larger to accept the ever increasing bounty of the Universe which is mine right now.

R

Forgiveness

Early on we introduced you to a four letter F word: fear. Now we want to introduce you to another F word, the lack of which is just as limiting, and whose importance misunderstood: Forgiveness.

From the viewpoint of Creative Force there is no such thing as forgiveness because Creative Force knows us only as perfect beings who sometimes forget our place within It. So what is to forgive? We cannot be forgiven by Creative Force because we have done nothing wrong which requires forgiveness. All we have to do is get back to the place of remembering our connection.

From our viewpoint as physical beings we get all muddled up in this concept of forgiveness. If we do something our spouse thinks is wrong we ask forgiveness. Sometimes it is granted, sometimes not. If we think another person has wronged us we may want them to ask our forgiveness, which we may or may not grant: frankly sometimes it is just about them asking us for forgiveness. In almost every instance the idea of asking for forgiveness or granting forgiveness has to do with our own perception of something being wrong. Isn't it interesting that with this forgiveness thing we are asking more of each other than Creative Force, the Supreme Source of our beings, asks of us? Maybe we could lighten up a bit on demanding others seek our forgiveness, you think?

In truth if someone does something to us we think is wrong and we refuse to forgive them, we are not hurting that other person, we only hurt ourselves. We carry around this huge sack of experiences we have not forgiven, or released from our lives. That sack is not weighing on those who "wronged us" it is weighing on us! It is our burden, and it grows heavier each time we add another item to the bag until we can scarcely move. Unforgiveness is a poison we are administering to ourselves.

Among the things this poison does: it results in physical illnesses, estranges us from friends and family, and produces more of its own poison. Most importantly to this discussion, unforgiveness closes off the path for delivery of the good we seek in our lives. Giving and receiving are a balance issue: if we do not give we cannot receive.

With unforgiveness, we are living in judgment of others, no matter how "right" we are about the issue, we still remain in judgment. As long as we are in judgment we are out of our own power. Being out of our own power is so crippling to our Spiritual selves we simply cannot be present to receive the good the Universe wants to deliver to us. So you see we are not hurting anyone else by being judgmental or unforgiving, the only one who truly gets injured is ourselves. We are fully in control of this cycle.

Forgiveness and forgetfulness are not the same thing. If someone has caused you physical harm, such as hitting you with their car, you do not have to forget the impact, or its repercussions and healing time: that is not necessarily placing us out of our place of power. But forgiving the other person for the act is important because we were also part of the scenario. For some reason we chose to be part of that experience. When we accept our place in the event, when we accept it was part of our manifestation as well, then we simply must forgive the other person. We need not blame them or ourselves, we can simply accept there is a lesson (or a gift) we requested within this experience, and it has been delivered clearly and forcefully. So what is there to forgive?

This whole topic of forgiveness is a book in itself, so allow us to offer this one suggestion of how we can forgive others, and ourselves, and move on. Keep the lesson, love the person. In doing this we unburden ourselves and free up the pathways to receive our good, which far outweighs whatever slight someone else may have committed.

Forgive for the best reason of all: it is good for YOU!

If forgiveness is requested I offer it immediately and graciously knowing that in Creative Force there is only love.

Give it Up!

Along the path to receiving sometimes we get the idea our good will never arrive, and then we fall into the trap of trying to effort our good into being. This is when we must take a step back to remember Creative Force has no time table as we know it. Time, and for that matter space, are limitations created by humankind.

Our good comes through us via the Unlimited. It is natural to get a little frustrated when what we seek does not appear to have arrived. As a result of that frustration we tend to get out of our own power, spend too much time looking around for where our good is. We start defining the way it must come into our experience. How and where our good arrives is not our work. That is what we mean by efforting. When we attempt to effort our good into being we may find ourselves at the bus station when our ship comes in. Stated another way, when we effort we can find ourselves looking in all the wrong places for what is already ours.

What do we do at this point? GIVE IT UP! Stop trying to force the how and where and when of the gifts Creative Force has already agreed to supply and relax into the receiving, in short, give it up.

This does not mean we give up on the good, it means we go back to our spiritual base, the connection we have; always have had, always will have, with Creative Force. It means relaxing and letting go of the steering wheel because you do not have to drive this bus. You can relax and know the good you seek is already here, but you may be looking in the wrong places and not recognize the gift for what it is! When we place a demand on Creative Force for say, a relationship which fills us with joy, one that provides emotional support, physical comfort, a reason to come home from work happy, Creative Force has an unlimited range of possibilities as to how this will be delivered. Now, let's take a look again at these demands: joy, emotional support, physical comfort. Somewhere in your mind you may have the idea these would all manifest as a man, handsome, self-reliant, employed, but what comes into your life is a puppy! The puppy fulfills all these demands just as you placed them into Creative Force. It is delivered, but because you had the preconceived notion it could only be delivered one way, you completely missed your gift, the complete and full manifestation of all your requests. You were at the bus station when your ship came in. We often neglect to be as specific as we might in our demands, and Creative Force isn't likely to send you an e-mail for clarification, It just does. If this happens to you, give it up, go back to step one and begin the Think, Believe, Receive process again. But, before you do that, remember to bless the arrival of your puppy, be grateful for the fulfillment of your request then begin again with enhanced clarity.

We cannot underscore the importance of gratitude as your part in the creative process of Think, Believe, Receive. Where we place our attention and energy grows. This means if we place our attention and energy in frustration that our gift has not arrived or that it arrived as a puppy rather than some movie hunk, we grow more frustration, not a movie hunk!

How does 'give it up' work for us? As we effort the manifestation of what we seek, we find ourselves further and further from its delivery. You have done your part in the thinking and believing, now do your part in the receiving. Do a mental inventory: puppy or no puppy have your demands for joy, emotional support, physical comfort and a reason to be happy when you come home after work manifested in your life? Have you have expressed your demand for these things and also honored your connection with Creative Force as the provider in your life? If you have, and It has, say thank you! The response to our demands may be physical, they may be emotional, they may be spiritual but they will always be met in the affirmative.

Now, if you still insist on a physical man to be part of your life, have you done your part to welcome him into your life? Have you given up trying to define how this desire will come into your life? Are you listening to your intuition? This is also a way in which your demand may be answered. Your intuition may lead you to accept an invitation to a party you had not planned to attend and maybe there you will meet Mr. Right; intuition may lead you to attend a girl's night out where this physical manifestation will be reveled. Just give it up!

Stop demanding what you want be delivered in a specific manner at a specific time. Give it up and go inside where the guidance to your good is always working and when you do this, go in an attitude of gratitude.

If your demand is for more prosperity it may manifest in a new job, or it may manifest in a new way of looking at your present job which leads to a promotion and more money. If you are asking for improved health it may come through a new prescription or it may come from relaxing in your life: stress is a major contributor to ill health. Creative Force is unlimited in the specifics of delivery. When we give it up we open ourselves to a wondrous array of possibility, we begin to live in the limitless possibility Creative Force knows.

To give it up is to commit yourself to the connection between yourself and Creative Force. To give it up removes from us the need to create, which is beyond our power anyway. The one most effective process in receiving is to reconnect with where your power truly lies, relax into knowing you do not have to effort this process, all you have to do is accept! Accept all the good in your life with gratitude, always with gratitude.

Where you place your attention grows. Place your attention in growing your faith of Creative Force in your life to deliver what you want. You will be amazed and delighted with the results.

My gifts are here for me now. I give it up and allow myself
to welcome those gifts into my life with gratitude.

The Vibrational Connection

We are Spiritual Beings having a physical experience. In Think, Believe, Receive we have already examined this in detail, just as we have discussed our belief that our physical manifestations (our bodies) are solid, then gone on to disproved this notion. We are not solid; we are made up of energy vibrating at specific frequencies which seem to be physical. So if we are not as we appear, what the heck are we? We are vibrational beings which have agreed to recognize our bodies as solid. We appear through vibrations, we send off vibrations, we receive vibrations and every other being on this level of creation does the same thing and together we agree on certain labels for those vibrational creations.

This vibrational reality has shown up in our lives constantly, usually in ways we can not give a name to, but intuit clearly. We are certain you can recall more than one situation where you have met a person for the first time and felt an immediate connection. At the same time you may have met a dozen other people, but only that one produced a special connection. We call this "vibrational resonance": a match-up in vibrational frequencies. You broadcast a vibration and this other person is broadcasting a vibration which resonates with yours. It is a wonderful feeling, isn't it?

The receiving process of Think, Believe, Receive is also vibrational. If you are broadcasting a vibration a vibration of fear you will only match those who are also broadcasting fear. If you are broadcasting a vibration of abundance, you will match up with abundance.

In the process of writing this chapter on vibrational connection I was delivered a wonderful gift by Creative Force— the perfect and clear demonstration of how our vibrational connection is present and working in our lives all the time. A young man by the name of Kevin approached me asking to borrow my cell phone because his was out of minutes. Kevin's story is a common one: his work evaporated after 9/11, his marriage fell apart, and child support was eating up what cash he had left and he suddenly found himself actually living on the streets. The previous night he had slept in the park. Still, his vibration as he approached me was one of hopefulness and this is what I felt from him. He was hopeful because he had a friend who could get him work if Kevin could reach him by telephone so I was delighted to assist him. As Kevin and I discussed the possibility of an improved financial experience for him his vibration was high and felt like a vibration I wanted in my life. Then, as he lapsed into his story of how he used to have a nice truck, stable home, great job, credit cards, all the trappings of the 21st century, then lost it all, his vibrational level plummeted. It was like a light had been turned off; No longer was Kevin living in possibility and positive expectation of a better life, of getting back to the life he wanted, he was sending off vibrations of despair and failure. If Kevin had approached me at that vibrational level, I would have done my best to assist him, but our vibrational connection would have been on a totally different level. I must honestly say I know my opinion of him would not have been as positive if this had been the level our first vibrational contact. That light that went off as Kevin spoke about what he had lost created a darkness around him, but all it takes to dispel darkness is light because darkness and lower vibrational emanations instantly vanish when light and our connection to Creative Force is present. Someone must have told you at one time or another to "Lighten up!" This is just what we do when we consciously live our life in the awareness of the vibrations we are sending out.

When we go out to find a new job, meet people, whatever it is we are doing, we can improve our relationships and increase possibility when we are conscious of our own vibrational broadcasts just as we are of those vibrations we receive. This is what Think, Believe, Receive is truly about: being conscious of our creative process be that process getting a better job, becoming more healthful, prosperous, finding a 'soul mate', all of these things are effect: the end result of our own vibrational broadcasts.

Have we just contradicted our often stated assertion that we do not create things ourselves, that we are just the receiver of these creations? No, and here is why: to receive any of the good stuff we want, and Creative Force has supplied, we must be in vibrational resonance with those things. How can we find peace when we approach life with a vibration of anger? It's not possible. How can we find prosperity when our vibration is one of lack? There is no way to do it. If we are not a vibrational match to what we say we want, even though that thing is right in front of us, it is invisible to us because we do not have a vibrational match up, a resonance with it. Are we suggesting love has a vibration? Yes indeed. Does this mean money has a vibration? Yes, but more importantly we must be vibrationally open to money coming into our lives. Does joy have a vibration? Yes, but again the more important understanding is that we must be vibrationally open to that joy for it to manifest in our lives.

Have you ever gone looking for your car keys and couldn't find them? You search the house top to bottom, once, twice, three times and still no keys. "I can't find my keys anywhere!" you declare. Guess what; this is all about vibrational connection. You have declared you cannot find your keys so your vibrational setting confirms this declaration, just as Creative Force does. Then someone else walks in and asks why you are so frazzled. "I can't find my keys" you reply, but they just look down at that end table you know you have examined unsuccessfully at least three times for those darn keys and they say, "Here they are!". Car keys, just as with all creation, do have a vibrational level. The most important aspect of this search is to be in the vibrational awareness that you can see those keys. In any search, for car keys, the perfect relationship, joy, health, sobriety, peace, happiness, contentment, you must align your vibrational level with what you seek to find.

How does this alignment come into being? From our experience we find the most effective way to align ourselves with what we are seeking is to move out of the negative approach (I.E. I can't find my keys) to the affirmative approach- I am finding those keys now! Such a tiny shift in vibration opens huge doors. Apply this approach to anything you are seeking: I know (fill-in the blank) is here, and I open myself to connecting with it now.

Vibrational resonance is working in us on so many levels right now simply because we are vibrationally constructed beings. That is one aspect of ourselves which will carry over into our next experience: we will always remain vibrational. This is why our intuition is so powerful and accurate; intuition is working completely on the vibrational plane where it is unhampered by appearances.

Become more aware of your vibrational presence: what is going out and what is coming in and your ability to receive your desires is enhanced a thousand fold.

I am aware of my vibrational message and the messages of others
as I allow all I desire to come into my life in joy and gratitude.

The Unintentional Power of No

Now that we have explored our vibrational nature, let's move into the vibrational aspects of words: specifically the word no and its variations (not, can't, less, without, etc).

We have noted that as humans we are constantly placing demands on Creative Force. If we are ill, we want to feel better, if we are lacking cash, we want more money. Creative Force takes these demands and always responds in the affirmative, It does not understand the concept of no which is why when we include the word no in our demands Creative Force does not recognize it.

If we say 'I don't want to be sick anymore', what Creative Force recognizes us demanding is 'I want to be sick.' If we say 'no more violence' what Creative Force responds to is a request for more violence. Those words we use which are variations of no simply disappear. Such is the unintentional power of no. We think we are asking for one thing, yet what we are placing into consciousness, into our vibration, is just the opposite. We live in what has been called an 'inclusion based universe.' This means all things are added to as we make our demands, there is no subtraction. Does this remind you of your most recent attempts to lose weight? "I don't want to be overweight anymore" converts to "I want to be overweight" and pounds are added!

When we create affirmations (and affirm itself means to add support to) we always want to phrase them as a positive statement of our consciousness. We would decline to create an affirmation along the lines of "I know right here and now there is no war". What we would do is affirm "I know right here and now there is peace." Creative Force will always add support to what we demand as It acts to deliver the manifestation. Knowing this, and knowing that Creative Force cannot recognize not, no, less, without, or any words of that negation type, please be aware of what you are saying and insure your words are in sync with the guidelines of Creative Force.

Think, Believe, Receive is not about *what* to think: you are free to think any darn thing you want, what this book is about is *how* to think: how to think clearly with conscious intention so that your word will be more powerful as it merges with the Unlimited. Just as we have made it clear Creative Force always says yes to our demands and we have learned to use this truth for our expanded experience, so too must we learn effective communication with the Unlimited.

Perhaps you have heard the phrase 'What we resist persists'? This is an example of how Creative Force deals with the unintended power of no. When loving people gather to make a statement for peace they often fall into the trap of making up signs which say things like "No More War". Well meaning as they may be, the affirmation Creative Force hears and delivers is "More War". So rather than promoting peace they have inadvertently advocated the chaos of war. Mother Theresa has been quoted as saying she would not attend an anti-war rally, but if someone held a peace rally, she would be there. This wonderful woman knew about the unintended power of no in our lives.

If you were the focus of the attention of a bully in school, or even at work, undoubtedly some one has counseled you not to respond to the bully but rather 'kill them with kindness'. This is indeed the most effective manner in which to respond to aggression because what we resist persists. The more attention we give the bully, the more they bully. Killing them with kindness truly suggests we can eliminate (kill) the aggression with love. Two biblical quotes come to mind on the topic of being the target of aggression: 'love turneth away wrath' and 'turn the other cheek.' What we want to do is meet aggression, anger or fear with love because where we give our attention grows. This is just another version of the idea that what we resist persists; if we are giving our attention to the unwanted, by Law it must grow.

As we become conscious of the unintended power of no we become more positive in our own speech as well. Who among us wants to be shut down with the word or intent of no? We all want to be heard, have our ideas given the opportunity to blossom, but when we respond with no, those possibilities are closed down creating a rift between ourselves and others. The most successful negotiators know this secret of Creative Force even if they do not recognize why it works. To keep the lines of communication open clearly between ourselves and others, as well as between ourselves and Creative Force, it is important to make our wants known from the most positive perspective possible.

The unintended power of no makes itself known in our day to day lives constantly through its almost invisible ability to negate our best intentions and produce results which are far from our intent. Without intending to, we create resentment from those who feel they did not get their message across and without intending to we send demands to Creative Force which are the exact opposite of what we want. The unintended power of no is a relatively simple consciousness shift which will reap rewards far greater than we have ever imagined. 'No' is a disempowering word with unintended results, so leave no behind and affirm the affirmative in all you do and say.

Creative Force always says yes to me, so I always find
a yes way to speak with Creative Force.

R

The Greatest Story Teller Ever

If you were to name the greatest story teller ever, who would it be? Ernest Hemmingway, Mark Twain, Will Rodgers, Agatha Christie, Stephen King, maybe Alan Cohen? These are indeed all great story tellers to be sure, but the greatest story teller of all times is YOU.

You are the greatest story teller ever because you have created your life experience one story at a time. Even if the stories you have based your life upon were first told to you by others, you have incorporated them into your life and made them your stories, personalized them, given them three dimensions and added your own power. Perhaps as a child you attempted to play the piano and were told you had no musical ability. That story, told by others, became your story which you told and retold yourself and others repeatedly though your life. Now, this story is not simply a collection of words strung together to form a sentence uttered by others, it is a powerful force in your own life; so powerful that perhaps you have never even picked up a musical instrument again to put this story to the test.

If you were told , as I was as a small child, you have the gift of gab, the idea you could communicate with others easily came naturally to you because you told and retold yourself that story, made it yours, it came to be part of your definition of yourself to yourself and to others.

While others may hesitate to speak in public, you simply see no reason why not to speak. You are, after all the greatest story teller ever!

As we move though life we hear an uncountable number of words from others which simply become part of the background noise, easily forgotten. But when we hear something that we take personally, those words become part of us. But to make them define us, to shape how we think and act, we must take those personal words and the surrounding stories another step. We must make it our story for those words to define us. We must give it our personal power. WE must make it our story for those words to define us because we are the greatest story teller ever!

This story telling talent we all have comes into Think, Believe, Receive because it is the stories we tell ourselves that either open or close the gates to receiving. Follow along with me: I say "I know I am supported by and am part of the unlimited of Creative Force" then I say, "I believe whatever I demand is provided for me in the perfect manner at the perfect time and I am conscious of its arrival" (so far so good?) but then I tell my story: "and it won't be what I really want". The great story teller that we are has just shut down our good and made it impossible to receive what we want in order to preserve our story.

Everything about this creative process revolves around centering our consciousness on the Unlimited, on the possible being the definition of our lives, yet all it takes is an off-hand remark, taken from a story we don't necessarily truly believe, to close us off.

We are so powerful in our story telling that if we could harness that power and put it to work for us we would own Madison Avenue in weeks; not just the advertising agencies on Madison Avenue, I mean Madison Avenue itself, we are that powerful. So how do you want to use your powerful creative ability to tell stories? Do you want to tell stories which end up limiting you or do you want to tell stories which empower you? All it takes is attention to your words and thoughts.

To receive more abundantly, clearly and rapidly we want to make sure the stories we tell ourselves and the stories we tell about our selves are stories which affirm our true nature as well as what we want to experience.

You are the greatest story teller EVER, so tell the stories well, tell your stories with conscious intent to be all you are and all you hope to be.

I am the greatest story teller ever. Creative Force loves to hear me tell what I want to be, have and experience so It can deliver all my good.

The Law of Circulation

We want to introduce one final Law in this creative process of Think, Believe, Receive: the Law of Circulation. You may also know this as "what goes around comes around" or even "as we give, so we receive."

Back in our section about Believe we got into a discussion about "Gimme' My Stuff" concerning the idea that wanting more stuff is greedy because so many people have less than we do ourselves. Once again it is important to remember we cannot be poor enough to help anyone else, we cannot be homeless enough to house another. We can, however, help ourselves and others as we receive by remembering we do not live alone on this planet. We live with billions of other humans. As we expand our personal experience of receiving, gratefully more and more, we also expand the possibility of others receiving more too, simply by enlarging the size of the entire basket of good on a global basis.

In order to expand this basket we have the power of the Law of Circulation to help us along. For most of us this has translated into the idea that the more we get, the more we give but this is just as backwards as the idea that seeing is believing. In truth the more we give, the more we get!

In my first prosperity class I heard a story about a traveling preacher who moved about with his son speaking at whatever church they happened upon. One Sunday the preacher and his son entered a small rural church and seeing a donation box in the lobby the preacher deposited a dollar. After presenting an amazingly uplifting sermon to the grateful congregation the Pastor of the church thanked the preacher and told him: 'we are a small congregation, able to pay you only from the proceeds of our donation box in the lobby.' Whereupon the traveling preacher was presented with the entire contents of the donation box: one dollar. As the preacher and his son made their way down the road the son said: "too bad you didn't put more money in the donation box, you would have gotten more out!"

The more we commit to a project, the more we receive from that effort. The receiving is not always tangible, sometimes we are repaid in the esteem of our peers or employers, but we always get as we give. Athletes who take the field and give 110% effort always stand out from those who simply show up for the game. Sometimes they get more pay for their efforts right away, sometimes not. But they always receive the benefit of their consciousness. If we do not commit ourselves fully to the creative process of Think, Believe, Receive we do not get full benefit. As we give, so we receive, the Law of Circulation in action. This applies to relationships, spirituality, joy, abundance, everything. The more we give the more we get.

Many of us want more money in our lives. Can we utilize the Law of Circulation in this quest? You bet! When we give to charity we are saying to Creative Force 'I have prosperity, I see prosperity in my life'. Law of Attraction kicks-in and picks up on the vibration of 'I have prosperity' and produces in our lives ever more prosperity. By the same token if we give to charity from the vibration of 'I hardly have enough for myself, but here's my money', Law of Attraction hears 'I am coming from lack' and mirrors back more lack.

Giving is essential to our prosperity and abundance in all things, BUT, giving must always come from an attitude of abundance. The Law of Circulation gives back based upon our vibrational base. The more we give, and give freely, joyously and from the vibration of abundance, the more Law of Circulation returns to us. Again, please remember, we do not give to receive, we receive as we give.

You have no doubt heard the homily that it is more blessed to give than to receive. I invite you now to expand on that idea: it is doubly blessed to give AND receive! Affirm to Creative Force that you understand that giving and receiving are parts of the same Law: the Law of Circulation, this is the power of giving.

Tithing is a form of giving too. Tithe means 10%. Many religions require a tithe of all members, and some go as far as to insist on reviewing congregants tax returns to insure their members' compliance. This is not tithing, nor giving, this is extortion. True giving, true tithing comes from an awareness of the Law of Circulation and how it functions in our lives. Money, right along with every other thing, seen and unseen, is vibration. For maximum return on our giving the vibration we want attached to the money we give— either as charity or tithing— to be a positive, affirmative vibration. The Laws of Circulation, Attraction, Cause and Effect, all respond to the vibration attached to giving: give from a vibration of lack, receive lack, give from a vibration of abundance, get more abundance, it's that simple. How much more powerful is a charitable contribution or tithe given from a vibration of abundance!

Edwene Gaines (we like to think of her as the Queen of Tithing) has a fabulous book called "The Four Spiritual Laws of Prosperity" we highly recommend. In this book Edwene says "Our tithes must go to those who have fed us spiritual food. We must not consider whether the recipients are rich or poor—that is not our concern. Our concern is to acknowledge our source by giving 10 percent to those who feed us spiritual food."

How joyful it is to recognize we are being fed spiritually, which in turn leads to more spiritual food, and so on. Once again the Laws of Attraction, Cause and Effect, Correspondence and Circulation come together powerfully and the result is greater than the sum of its parts. The results are multiplied exponentially if we conduct our tithing and charitable giving from a consciousness of awareness of how affirmative giving positively impacts on our lives.

As we give in a consciousness of cooperation with the Law, we find we can only give from love and abundance. We are no longer concerned that the homeless person to whom we give money will use it to purchase booze; we are no longer concerned with how the charity will use our money because we come from a place of love and abundance in our giving. Of course we use due diligence when giving to charity rather than support scam artists, but there are two factors to also remember: first is that because we are conscious of the guidance of Creative Force in our lives, we are always lead to the perfect recipient for our giving, and secondly we are not giving strictly for the benefit of others, we are giving—be it time or money— because we recognize that our willingness to give sets up in our own being a willingness to receive, and receive we will: full measure, packed down.

Work with the Law of Circulation— give from love and cooperation with Creative Force.

I give freely, knowing the extent of my receiving is mirrored in my willingness to give. I give, knowing I do receive.

Until Now

One of the things which holds back the receiving of our good is the idea we are, for lack of a better word, sinners, and therefore unworthy of all the good we can conceive because of our past actions. So let's look at that idea, the idea of sinning.

Simply put sinning is thinking and or acting outside our greatest good. We can trace the origin of the word sin to an old archery term "sine" which means to miss the mark. When we think and or behave in a manner inconsistent with our perfect nature we are missing the mark, that's all! When we forget we are perfect expressions of Creative Force, we miss the mark, and thereby, sin (or sine). For us, everything we can conceive is ours, yet we often adopt the idea we must earn or qualify for what we seek because of our previous actions and thoughts. What we are doing here is clearly missing the mark.

One of the aspects of the Catholic Church we so admire is the ritual of confession. Through the admission of our acts of sinning, or missing the mark as set forth in Scripture, or tradition, we can regain our position of worthiness. The first step is always to admit to ourselves- and then in the case of the Church, to a priest that we have fallen short of our goal. What is that goal? That goal is to love ourselves and others, just as Creative Force loves us. For some this is called being in a state of Christ Consciousness: the recognition that we are all one, and that to harm another is to harm ourselves. This act of contrition and absolution is a beautiful thing because it reflects perfectly how Creative Force views us. Of course for this ritual to be effective we must first be willing to honestly participate, rather than just do lip-service to the act.

Communion is also a ritual which re-connects us to our Source. In the case of Communion we recognize Jesus as our Point of Connection, Source, or Creative Force. Jews have their Day of Atonement, which encourages us to take stock of our actions and thoughts. Ritual sacrifice fulfills the same purpose as we seek blessings for ourselves and our endeavors; a re-connection to our oneness. Many Native American Traditions have some version of seeking blessings and re-establishing oneness with Creative Force through the ritual of saying prayers to each of the Cardinal points of the compass.

What all these rituals and traditions have in common is a recognition that we, as physical humans, do not always think and behave in accordance with our highest good. Through these rituals we can once again place ourselves, re-align ourselves with Creative Force regardless of the name we use for It.

If any of these traditions and rituals reflects your comfort zone, and they do the job for you— go in peace. Should you find yourself less than filled through these experiences we would like to offer another possibility which can also bring you back into alignment with Creative Force and unblock your receiving. One free of judgment and its accompanying guilt, blame and resultant blocks to your good.

Step one: admit to yourself that as a human being you have missed the mark in some way.

Step two: release this seeming shortcoming with love. After all you did the best you could at that moment, right?

Step three: Adopt the mantra 'Until Now'.

Until now I have not been as good a husband as I would like,

Until now I have focused more on my lack than my prosperity.

Until now I have not given or gotten what I seek from this situation.

Through the power of these two words 'Until Now' we recognize we have missed the mark- chosen to think or behave in a manner out of alignment with our highest good, and we recognize this truth in a clear, straight forward manner which absolves us of guilt or shame because at the same time we recognize we have more and better to give, and state our intention to do just this.

Until now math has been a problem for me.

Until now I have consumed more food than is good for me and my goals.

Until now sobriety has been beyond my grasp.

Until now this person has been an irritant to me.

Until now means we recognize what has been our behavior has been, and that from here on out we recognize our choice in the matter to approach the situation differently. (This is a good opportunity to go back and review the chapter called **Now, Now, Now** and remember where and when our power is.)

Why does this simple phrase until now have so much power? Until now works for us just the same way as forgiveness does. What we are doing is forgiving ourselves our past shortcomings and opening the door to a better future: simple words, simple process. Remember, Creative for does not know precedence, or what has come before. Creative Force only knows now. Even if for 50 years your thought has been one of separation from Creative Force and your power, right now, this instant, you can re-align with your power, right now you can come back into love— for yourself and others. Nowhere is there a big book which contains details of your every peccadillo or inability to do this or that. There is no one keeping score on your inability—until now— to solve algebraic equations, to eat appropriate amounts of food, get along with others and just waiting for the opportunity to hold you accountable. You, and only you have been writing that big book yourself!

Creative Force only knows now. That is the power of the term Until Now, and why is works so simply. Creative Force knows now, so as you integrate the idea of Until Now into your thought process, every good thing you wish to experience, every change of thought and action you wish to embody, can and will be yours to manifest.

Until Now releases us to move forward in experiencing the life we wish to experience. That hasn't been possible- Until Now!

I release any limitation I have created Until Now and move forward with Creative Force to a more rewarding future.

Checklist for Receive

1) I allow the gifts I have requested to manifest in my life with ease and love.

2) I have created a space in my life to receive the good which is already mine.

3) I forgive myself and others with equal ease because I know in Creative Force giving forgiveness is essential to receiving.

4) I release the urge to control how my good comes into my life, and allow Creative Force to deliver perfectly, on time, every time.

5) I have aligned my vibration with the vibration of what I seek, and do so in love, joy and peace at all times.

6) I understand the unintentional power of no and place my demands on Creative Force from the affirmative always.

7) I am the greatest story teller ever, so I tell the story the way I want it to be.

8) I give, knowing this is part of my spiritual commitment and commitment to myself.

9) I embrace the truth that my life is better, no matter what has happened, "Until Now"

TBR

In Conclusion

We have presented 27 individual chapters so far in Think, Believe, Receive, this will be number 28. We know this might seem overwhelming to the new truth voyager who has, until now, not considered a conscious approach to creating the life they want for themselves. Please release any fear around these individual topics. Taken as a whole these chapters form an interlocking network to help us create in a manner which is in alignment with the Laws of Creative Force. One does not have to fully enact all 28 at one time; simply allow them to be guideposts for your spiritual awakening. You may already be aware of and practicing some of these ideas anyway.

We are eternal, vibrational, spiritual beings having the physical experience we have chosen this time around. Be easy on yourself, this life is a process, there is no pass-fail grading system here—Creative Force loves us simply because we are. You are living your perfect experience one step at a time.

The life you are experiencing is a direct result of every human experience since the first Hominid took a step in the grasslands of Africa, and in truth this trail goes back even further; every step of upgrading from single cell to multiple cells, every advancement in technology of gathering food and finding shelter has been a step by step creation. Our lives and what we experience are the result of every desire of every person who has ever walked this planet seeking better nutrition, better housing, easier transportation, more creature comforts, and more safety. These things did not just appear at a single moment as if out of thin air, their very existence owes everything to those who have come before us, so don't sweat the small stuff, things are still getting better.

Thee hundred years ago most of the world's population lived and died at the whim of a Monarch. Starvation was the norm; childhood mortality was such that the death of a new born was a universal occurrence regardless of one's station in life. Today Monarchs who can bring about the death of a subject on a whim are almost non-existent. While malnutrition still exists on our planet it is the result of conditions brought about by fear (and we have learned what that truly is and how to deal with it in our own lives). Hunger, malnutrition, unnecessary infant mortality are within our ability to erase right now, and all this in a short 300 years! This is a truly remarkable accomplishment and it is the direct result of the consciousness of humankind combining from their individualistic perspectives to create a better life for all. You are part of that change, and now you can do it intentionally, consciously, and with greater power.

The pace of improvement is quickening, and through the creative process of Think, Believe, Receive you are part of that quickening advancement in a heightened manner, from awareness rather than ignorance.

Yes, injustice still exists, yes hunger is still a physical reality, yes fear in the form of warfare, greed and disregard for our own planet can still be found, yet these are no longer taken for granted. We no longer refer to them simply as 'God's Will' or "the way things are" or the dreaded "That's just reality". Today as never before we are coming to see ourselves as we truly are: part of the whole, a dynamic, wonderful web of Oneness. This Oneness insures our individuality, actually it insists upon our individuality to create and then takes our creativity and makes it manifest. The result of this exchange is more respect for ourselves, our neighbors, people in other countries, our planet and yes, even our Universe. Yet it all begins in one place, and that place is within us. Each individual creates a new piece of the experience. Remember, it is not possible to create more prosperity, more safety, and more joy for ourselves without at the same time creating more of the same for every soul on this planet: two legged; four legged, crawling, swimming or flying. It is simply not possible to improve the conditions for one without creating improved conditions for all.

As we let go of fear, of lack and limitation, warfare, hunger, and brutality we let go of every aspect of the human condition which is absent in Creative Force. We do not have to eliminate each of these aspects through our personal experience one by one, we don't have to create a matrix to deal with them in order, we don't have to even be aware of the word for each and every issue, all we have to do is lend our raised consciousness to the improvement.

That four letter "F" word, fear, leads us to do things which are other than life affirming, from the smallest interactions to cosmic interactions. As we move forward in love and conscious, awareness that we are all one; as we know we are all in our perfect place, when we heed the words of every illumined being ever to be recorded: to love each other as we love ourselves, fear dissolves.

This may seem too large a proposition to take on, but to paraphrase Robert Kennedy: If not you, who? If not now, when? Step by step this process evolves, expands and manifests in every life with joy. So how do we begin? Through our own individual consciousness.

THINK: HOW CAN IT BE BETTER
BELIEVE THERE IS A FORCE WHICH
SUPPORTS YOU IN THAT DESIRE
RECEIVE THE FRUITS OF YOUR DESIRES.

It all begins with you, right now.

I now move forward consciously knowing I can live a better life. Creative Force fully supports me in that desire, so I welcome into my life only the best possible experiences.

Bibliography

Bowen, Will, A Complaint Free World, copyright 2007 Published by Doubleday

Gaines, Edwene, The Four Spiritual Laws of Prosperity, copyright 2005, Published by MJF Books.

Holmes, Ernest, The Science of Mind, copyright 1938, Published by Tarcher/Putnam

Glossary of terms
used in Think, Believe, Receive

Cause Creative Force in it's purest form: pure potential.

Christ Consciousness Love God, and love your neighbor as yourself.

Consciousness awareness, consciousness is the pathway to maximize creativeness.

Creative Force also known as God, Spirit, First Cause, The Universe, Allah, The Force, along with many other names including Chuck.

Creative Medium the medium through which Creative Force produces effects

Demand our thought impress on Creative Force.

Dogma belief apart from conscious thought. Ideas accepted but not examined.

Effects what comes about as a result of the creation of Creative Force.

Fear finding excuses and restraints. The reasons we generate to not live our lives fully.

Integrity Having and living a code of conduct based upon Christ Consciousness

Love the true being of Creative force. Through love all is manifested.

Manifestation the result of Creative Force producing.

Omnipotence The All Powerful One. Creative Force.

Omniscience The All-Knowing, All-Perceiving Mind of Creative Force.

Omnipresence Creative Force is everywhere present.

Race Consciousness ideas we accept from the whole experience of all life.

Religion traditions and dogma which have an original basis of spirituality.

Spiritual that part of ourselves which is in constant and direct contact with Creative Force.

Thought is based on what we think, and powerful to the extent we infuse it with feeling and emotion.